# Worship Leader Handbook

Rod E. Ellis

Unless otherwise indicated, Scripture quotations are from The Holy Bible, New Living Translation, © 1996, 2004, 2015 by Tyndale House Foundation.

# DEDICATION

*For Jackie, my favorite worshiper.*

# CONTENTS

# ACKNOWLEDGMENTS

This book is a group project, perhaps bigger than most. The group called "family" gave up a lot to make this possible. I couldn't have done this without Jackie, Catherine or Emily. Our older daughter, Catherine, spent hours checking and fixing grammar and formatting.

Then there's the group called "Worship Leader Academy" at Woodburn Baptist Church. In multiple ways, they helped me write the content as we explored each subject together.

And there is the group of churches I have had the pleasure to learn from, and that have served as a the laboratory for the development of these ideas: Karl Road Baptist in Columbus, OH; FBC Lansdale, PA; Mt Carmel BC Cincinnati, OH; Memorial BC Frankfort, KY; Woodburn BC Woodburn, KY; and for shorter periods of time, Latonia BC Covington, KY; Journey Baptist Fellowship Lexington, KY; and Immanuel BC Lexington, KY.

Other groups and leaders were even more foundational, especially the classes and professors at The Southern Baptist Theological Seminary between 1988 and 1991. The words of great teachers Milburn Price, John Dickson, and Donald P. Hustad ring from these pages.

My pastor, Dr. Tim Harris of Woodburn Baptist Church has and is forming my soul and life in ways I never thought I would be experiencing this far into my journey. Of course none of this would be possible or mean anything without my earthly parents, Kaye Ellis and Jim and Fran Ellis. How much more my heavenly Father! If there's any truth in this effort it comes from Him.

# 1 — INTRODUCTION

I've been wanting to write a book for a long time.

But it intimidates the daylights out of me. In many ways, writers are my heroes. When I meet someone who has written a book, I think of them as special—typically the kind of person I aspire to be. And so when I started writing, it was a sort of wake up call. I'm not the kind of person I aspire to be, let alone the kind of person you should aspire to be. I'm just a guy who wants to share some things that I've learned in an effort to serve others who are striving to raise up servant leaders for worship ministry.

I also have this conviction that I shouldn't just write my spin on what everyone else is writing. And so finally, a project came to mind that seems to fill an empty space in the conversation. Since I've not found any such resource for how a worship pastor in a "normal" church can help raise up the next generation of worship leaders, I thought it might be time to offer my voice to the marketplace of ideas in worship ministry.

From everything I can see, there seems to be a shortage of godly, thoughtful, skilled, passionate, people-loving worship leaders in the United States. While I would never claim to be all of those things most of the time, I have been told that I am at least some of those things some of the time. In writing this book I have experienced challenge after challenge that makes me yearn to exhibit most of those characteristics more often.

I was aware of this worship leader shortage a few years ago, but it wasn't until I came to serve at Woodburn Baptist Church (about 10 miles south of Bowling Green, KY; 70 miles north of Nashville, TN) that this became a passion for me. In 2005, our church embraced a 20/20 Vision, to plant 20 church by 2020. At the time, WBC was running about 400 in worship. Ours is not a mega-church, but it is a great church with a mega-vision.

When the church asked me to be their worship pastor, it was clear from my job description, the interview process, and conversations since: I was being asked to prepare worship leaders to be part of planting churches. Having lived in that vision for 2-3 years now, it occurs to me this involves not just a "worship leader" but the whole worship ministry. If we plant a church with 75-100 people, they probably need a few musicians and a few tech servants. And they need to be men and women who are godly, thoughtful, skilled, and passionate. More importantly, they must love people!

That's why we created our Worship Leader Academy. This is a 16 session, quasi-school journey designed to equip emerging worship leaders to lead a song, a service, or a ministry. It was conceived to be a place where we could start preparing people of all ages to be ready to be part of a ministry of church planting. This isn't the only step our worship ministry has taken to serve our "20/20 Vision," but it is a key one. Our first year we had nine people walk through the material. They are a huge part of the pages that follow. They helped shape it. In some cases, their contribution is exactly what you see on the page. I am so grateful for Thomas, Isabelle, Joshua, Vicki, Jason, Emma, Sam, Shannon, and Margie.

My suggestion is that you use this book to walk one or more people in your church through a similar process. It could be a powerful one-on-one experience for a worship pastor and their mentee. My hope is that it will often be used as a small group resource, for existing worship leading groups, or for your own organization that functions somewhat like our Academy experience. (See Appendix A for more about our Worship Leader Academy experience.)

If you encounter anything in this book that doesn't ring true, that could be clarified or improved, or if you have questions not addressed in the book, please contact me at RodEEllis@gmail.com. Or look me up on Facebook. I'd love to connect with you.

One more thing: after writing about how a worship ministry should be taught, I am aspiring to make my ministry be more like the one that is described in these chapters. I don't want you, the reader, to think being a part of our ministry at Woodburn is shiny and perfect. Overall, it is certainly healthier than others I've led, but we are far from ideal. We are striving to have great relationships with God and each other, great rehearsals, and great services. Sometimes we come close. Sometimes we fall short. The words of the apostle Paul ring true:

> *"I don't mean to say that I have already achieved these things or that I have already reached perfection. But I press on to possess that perfection for which Christ Jesus first possessed me. No, dear brothers and sisters, I have not achieved it, but I focus on this one thing: Forgetting the past and looking forward to what lies ahead, I press on to reach the end of the race and receive the heavenly prize for which God, through Christ Jesus, is calling us."* - Philippians 3:12-14

And I want to take as many with me as I can.

## 2 — LEADING YOURSELF

The truth is familiar: The hardest person you will ever lead is yourself.

And the most important.

If you lead yourself well, you can have a far greater impact on those around you. They will respect you. They will want to learn from you. They will want to be led by you.

And if you don't lead yourself well?

Less respect. Less teachable. Less willing.

~

Have you ever been on a plane? Maybe you fly so often the flight attendant's instructions are a nuisance rather than a survival guide. Either way, as they faithfully (and legally!) instruct us on every flight: it is essential that if you're traveling with someone dependent on you for help, you put the oxygen mask on yourself before trying to help them. If you can breathe, you can help a lot of folks who can't. But if you can't breathe, you can't help a single person. Even your own child.

What makes sense on a plane often gets overlooked in the busyness of daily life.

Put your oxygen mask on first. Lead yourself well. Only then you will be in a position to lead others well.

Rory Noland has taught me a great deal. My first connection with him was through the significant book, *Heart of the Artist*. Later I learned that he was music director at Willow Creek for 20 years and worship pastor at Harvest Bible in Chicago. Rory once said to me that I needed to learn to exercise the muscle called "self leadership." I quickly followed up with a question, "At nearly 50 years of age, how in the world do I learn to do that?" His answer was worth the price of his salad at Applebee's that day: accountability.

You can learn more about Rory at www.heartoftheartist.org.

Want to go to the gym more? Get a workout buddy. Want to eat better? Find a nutrition support system—like Weight Watchers. Want to worship better? Be part of a small group that shares your goal. You might even work through this book with a small group of folks who yearn to find ways to connect the heart of God with the hearts of people. (See Appendix 1.)

There are at least 4 key areas of self leadership required for effective worship leaders: Spiritual Disciplines, Position Development, Self Awareness, and Submission to Authority.

## SPIRITUAL DISCIPLINES

*Don't you realize that in a race everyone runs, but only one person gets the prize? So run to win! All athletes are disciplined in their training. They do it to win a prize that will fade away, but we do it for an eternal prize.* - 1 Corinthians 9:24-25

*Something is wrong if you find that any discipline or habit you practice is making you arrogant, self-righteous, contemptuous, judgmental...* Mark Buchanan in *Your God Is Too Safe*

Athletes use discipline to run a race. And to win.

As important as training is to an athlete, it is infinitely (and eternally!) more important for us to use discipline to explore the Presence of the God, especially when we have been entrusted to lead others to worship. The stakes are higher in

> *We practice spiritual disciplines to develop intimacy with our Father.*

the spiritual realms. I need this reminder often: if an Olympian spends hours every day training to win a medal that will fade, how imperative it is that I learn to spend every breath in pursuit of godliness that can impact people for eternity.

This is essential: We practice spiritual disciplines to develop intimacy with our Father. We don't do it because we're supposed to, or so we can compete with other Christ-followers, or so we can get a jewel in our crown. If the reward of God's presence is not enough incentive or reward, we're doing it wrong. It's sort of like the figure skater I saw one weekend: she demonstrated that she was stronger than me, but strength got in the way of her grace.

So can ours.

There are many, many fine books, articles, blogs, podcasts, etc. on spiritual disciplines. For our purposes I have chosen to use Richard Foster's list of twelve. Here they are with my admittedly over-simplified description of each:

**The Inward Disciplines**
- Meditation — Filling your mind with a single, profound thought of our faith (e.g. the great love of God)
- Prayer — Conversation with God
- Fasting — Denying yourself something—usually food and/or drink—in order to have focused time of communion with God
- Study — Using resources to dive deep into a scripture verse or passage

**The Outward Disciplines**

- Simplicity — Choosing to live on less
- Solitude — Time alone, in quietude
- Submission — Giving up authority
- Service — Doing something for someone else while expecting nothing in return

**The Corporate Disciplines**
- Confession — Telling another trustworthy Christ-follower about sin in your life
- Worship — Focusing all of your attention and affection on God
- Guidance — Asking others to pray for direction or a decision in your journey
- Celebration — Expressing joy over something God has recently done

One of the reasons I appreciate Foster's *Celebration of Discipline* approach so much is that he suggests we tackle these one at a time. This year, for example, why don't you focus on one discipline you are already doing pretty well? Take it from good to great. Then next year—for the whole year—add just one. The next year, add another. Ask our Father to help you discern which to tackle next.

Increasingly I hear people talking about "soul care." There are many great resources available to help you care for your soul, but the one I've found most helpful is people who will sit with me and tell me the truth. One of my closest friends now lives many hours away, but we used to meet regularly over lunch and ask each other, "How is your soul doing?" Self leadership is fueled by the loving input of fellow journeyers.

~

INDIVIDUAL CHALLENGE — Read enough about each of the classic disciplines to determine which you will use as a path to intimacy with the Father this year. Remember, a few small steps in the right direction is the most lasting way to change. Start with something you think you will excel at doing. If you're already doing several of these (with joyful, glad obedience), choose one you've not yet tackled. If they have become tasks to be checked off rather than a path to intimacy, drop one so you can slow down the tasks in order to pursue the relationship.

GROUP CHALLENGE — Share your chosen discipline for the year with the group. At the beginning of each class/ gathering, take no more than 90 seconds to share how each of you are doing. If your group has more than 12, break into smaller groups to share. Be the accountability partners that will help strengthen the muscle of self-leadership.

## POSITION DEVELOPMENT

*"Work willingly at whatever you do, as though you were working for the Lord rather than for people."* - Colossians 3:23

*"Learning is the master skill of leadership."* - Kouzes/Posner

I want to be better.

Whatever my role is, I want to do better at it next month than I am this month. If you are an artist—musical, technical, dramatic, visual, or public speaker—I suspect you do too. And next year? I want to have improved enough that it impacts the way I carry out my role. Are you a drummer? Then by all means, find a way to get better. You will make everyone around you better. Do you play guitar or keys? Refine your skills. It will inspire those around you to do the same. Do you sing or speak? Find ways next month to use your voice better than you did last month.

No one can do this for you. It's the muscle of self-leadership.

Think back for a minute to when you first picked up your instrument. Remember how awkward it felt? How your fingers wouldn't do what your brain told them to do? How thankful were you that the sounds that came out of that instrument were only audible to you, not your family and friends? How did you get better?

Self-leadership. That is the "muscle" you used to practice.

You kept finding ways to work the scales on the piano, or change positions on the fretboard, or make sure every note was on pitch. The difference between then and now is--quite likely--astounding.

Don't stop now.

Psalm 33:3 says plainly: "play skillfully... and sing with joy."

We will explore this more deeply later, but excellence at your position matters. No one else can make you great at what you do. That's up to you. Bob Kauflin wrote in *Worship Matters*, "Don't practice 'til you get it right, practice until you can't get it wrong." When you do this, you will discover that by developing your position in the team, you will find greater freedom to worship and far greater freedom to lead others to worship.

This means improving your general skills, of course. But it also means preparation for rehearsals and services. This is one of the ways the world of worship leading has changed dramatically. Back in the day, we came together to learn songs. Now we come together knowing our part of the songs, excited to see what happens when the team—singers,

> *"Sing a new song of praise to Him; play skillfully on the harp, and sing with joy."*
> ~ Psalm 33:3

instrumentalists, and technicians—make music. The possibilities are so much greater when every person on the team continues to get better and better.

INDIVIDUAL CHALLENGE — Identify one strength and one weakness, two skills you'd like to improve in your role during the length of this study and share it with your group. Lean into your strengths, and make them stronger. Identify your weaknesses, and shore them up. For the drummer, it might be rudiments or tempo. For the keyboard player, it may be playing in sharps instead of flats or more sharps/ more flats. For the guitar player, it may be navigating key changes or playing more complex chords. For the singer, it might be attention to dynamics or physical expression. For the screens tech, it might be learning the next level of graphic design or attention to detail. For the sound tech, identifying specific pitches and their corresponding frequency or a mechanism for serving those on the platform. For the ministry leader it could be writing, helping you articulate your vision more clearly. For anyone, it might be the freedom to worship while serving on the platform.

GROUP CHALLENGE — Check in with one another periodically to see how you are improving. Don't just talk about it when you're together, though. Encourage one another. Cheer each other on. When you notice that someone else is improving, tell them. When everyone does this, everyone is built up. Use this exercise as a way to foster a culture of mutual encouragement.

## SELF-AWARENESS

*Examine yourselves to see if your faith is genuine. Test yourselves.* 2 Corinthians 13:5

*If we are to be great artists, we must remember we are His art. If we are to become gifted storytellers, we must first be aware of our part in the Story.* - Jeff Parker (quoted in *Pursuing Christ. Creating Art* by Gary Molander)

It is difficult to lead yourself well if you don't know yourself well.

And it is difficult to know yourself well if you only know yourself through your own lens.

Preacher Andy Stanley is fond of saying that some sins are hard to see in the mirror. I'd add that some strengths are hard to see there too. And so, ironically, one of the keys to self awareness is using instruments and other people to understand yourself.

There are dozens of helpful resources here: Myers-Briggs Personality Test, the DISC Inventory, Strengthfinder, S.H.A.P.E. (from Saddleback Church), Enneagrams, etc. The choice of which tool to use is less important than the choice to use one.

A mentor of mine, Karl Babb, once took me to lunch. (Should've been the other way around!) He asked me a question that caught me off guard: "You don't have any idea how weird you are, do you?"

Yeah, I laughed too.

And then my feelings were a little hurt, so I listened with a tender heart. He asked how many of the 90 other churches in the region where I'd faithfully served for 7 years would be likely to hire me. I could think of 2, and one was in a different denomination. I am weird!

Guess what? So are you! You just don't know it because you've only known your life from inside your own head. Actually, in many ways, you're also not weird at all. And that's one of the reasons I like the Myers-Briggs for this sort of thing. It helps us all realize there are a lot of people with the same personality traits, and that every personality has tremendous value to add to the team.

But you can't know this without self-awareness.

I'd like to take this to another level, though. There are things about yourself that you will only know as God reveals them to you. Consider the song lyrics of ancient Israel:

*Search me, O God, and know my heart;*
*test me and know my anxious thoughts.*
*Point out anything in me that offends you,*
*and lead me along the path of everlasting life.*
Psalm 139:23-24

Self-awareness also means knowing what is offensive in us. We are clothed in the righteousness of Christ because our sin is only cured by His covering. There is still—and always will be—sin in us.

As we develop in the spiritual disciplines, as we walk with others on this faith journey, as we seek to continually improve, we might have less sin. More likely, though, we will have less outward sin, the stuff others can't see. But we will always be sinning and in need of our Savior.

Paul wrote it plainly to the church in Rome: "Don't think you are better than you really are. Be honest in your evaluation of yourselves, measuring yourselves by the faith God has given us." (Romans 12:3b)

Why does this faith-gift matter so much?

I'll offer three reasons: 1) It fuels our worship; 2) It combats power struggles on the team; 3) It diffuses the temptation to arrogance that comes "under the lights."

It fuels our worship. Remember the story of the woman and her alabaster jar in Luke 7:36-50? If not, you might take a minute to go read it. It's the story of a religious leader and an immoral woman in the presence of Jesus. That's right, both are in the presence of Jesus. Simon is unaffected, unmoved…except he moves toward judgmentalism. The the immoral woman "kept kissing his feet and putting perfume on them." I'd rather be the one at the feet of Jesus than the one condemning the one at His feet. I imagine you would too.

It combats power struggles. Having been on the winning side and the losing side of power struggles among serious-minded Christ followers, I'd have to say there is actually no winning side. None. On the other hand, when we all come to a conversation or a decision not thinking of ourselves as better than we are, the only power that matters is the power of the Spirit. When you think you're better than your teammate, your team is in trouble. Not better on guitar, or sound, or fiddle. Just better. Another verse that helps me here is Philippians 2:3, "Don't be selfish; don't try to impress others. Be humble, thinking of others as better than yourselves."

Yes, I said a verse that helps me. I don't know of anyone who is can honestly say this isn't a struggle. It might be inward more than outward, but this is one of those challenges that is "common to mankind." Self leadership in authentic community will make a massive difference in our effectiveness.

Finally, the kind of faith that God gives us diffuses temptations toward arrogance. As a seasoned worship leader, I can tell you that people who aren't on the platform, who aren't under the lights, often perceive those of us who lead as arrogant. Sometimes they're right. It takes enormous confidence to stand in front of people, whether dozens or thousands, and reveal your artistic skills. That confidence can be misperceived as pride. But the lights, the recognition (or downright fame), and the admiration can easily lead to a haughty spirit. When we humble ourselves before God and one another, we can diffuse both arrogance and the perception of it.

~

## FASHION

The way you dress for leading worship should communicate something very clearly: this is not about you. This is about "jars of clay" or "earthen vessels" (2 Corinthians 4:7) who are nothing special but contain something supernaturally special. Dress modestly. Ladies, if you think there's a chance it is too short or too revealing, it is. If your grandmother would think it is too short or too revealing, it is. Gentlemen, dress nicely but don't be flashy. For all of us, the goal is not to draw attention to ourselves. In fact, the goal is to *not* draw attention to ourselves.

If this seems a little over the top, consider the regulations for the worshiping community of Israel in Exodus 20:26, specifically the "proper use of altars" where the instruction was, "Do not approach my altar by going up steps. If you do, someone might look up under your clothing and see your nakedness." I laughed when I really saw that for the first time. But then it struck me: God wants no distraction, no humiliation of His people, no chance for the "attention and affection" of the worshiper to be placed on anyone but Him. He is a jealous God.

INDIVIDUAL CHALLENGE — Take a personality inventory or similar assessment. Something more thorough and more credible than whatever version is going around social media is probably in order. If you aren't sure where to start, ask your pastor, a psychologist, or a business leader in your circle of friends. Learn something about yourself you didn't already know.

GROUP CHALLENGE — Discover how your personality profile interacts with someone else on the team. If possible, find out the profile of your leader (band leader, worship pastor, pastor), and learn how your profiles are likely to interact.

ADVANCED CHALLENGE — Learn enough about the ways personalities play off of one another to be able to maneuver through conflict. Remember, as Max Lucado says, "Conflict is inevitable. Combat is optional."

## SUBMISSION TO AUTHORITY

*Out of respect for Christ, be courteously reverent to one another.* Ephesians 5:21 - The Message

*If you can't follow well, you will make a poor leader. The greatest leader ever to walk this earth was a follower. The Savior submitted himself to the Father and followed his will.* - Aubrey Malphurs in *Being Leaders*

We lead best when we follow well.

A few years ago, I was privileged to spend a good deal of my time with various worship pastors and lead pastors in my part of the country. I enjoyed so much getting to hear of the victories they shared. Conversely, I was saddened so deeply by learning how much strife there "usually is" between these two leadership positions.

Brothers and sisters, this should not be so.

I know... it's always the other staff member's fault. Maybe. But maybe not. Maybe those of us in the lead musician role think we ought to be in the lead pastor role. Or maybe the lead singer thinks they should be the worship leader. Or perhaps the best musician in the group thinks they would be the best leader in the group.

And these dynamics are all wrapped up in two verses of scripture I have come to cherish, even when it means I don't get my way.

The first is about all relationships in the body of Christ. Ephesians 5:21 is clear: "Submit to one another out of reverence for Christ." Have you seen this in action? It is beautiful. It is powerful! Mutual submission is key to mutual edification. When you gladly submit, others are built up. And in the sweet mystery of our faith, when you gladly submit, you are built up too. This works in your marriage. It works in your ministry. It works in a band and in a choir. It works everywhere.

A second verse is specific in regard to the leadership of a pastor. Hebrews 13:7 is clear too: "Obey your spiritual leaders, and do what they say...Give them reason to do this with joy and not with sorrow."

Whatever role you find yourself in on your team, would you say your spiritual leader's joy is increased by the way you serve? If you are the volunteer, part-time, or full-time staff person charged with leading the worship ministry in your church, does your pastor smile at your work or grimace when you walk in the room? Band member, sound or screens operator, when your Minister of Music or Worship Pastor sees you in the rotation for a Sunday, does she or he look forward to you being there, or is there sorrow in their heart because of the way you will interact before, during, and after rehearsals and services?

Self-leadership.

The person in authority can't make these attitude choices for you. You have to learn to exercise the muscle of self leadership. If you struggle here, find an accountability partner. Vent your frustrations to Jesus before you have to release them to those who are your spiritual leaders.

Many scholars think one of the first hymns sung by the followers of Jesus is found in Philippians 2. The phrase just before those lyrics should inform worship leaders of every kind: "You must have the same attitude that Christ Jesus had." And then the song that follows is all about how Jesus chose submission. Jesus did. God in flesh chose to give up divine privilege. How far did His attitude take him? To a criminal's death on a cross.

Jesus led Himself well. And it led to His death.

"My old self has been crucified with Christ. It is no longer I who live, but Christ lives in me." (Galatians 2:20)

Honestly, I wonder how many souls have been wounded or lost while pastors and worship pastors were fighting over who was in charge. The middle of Hebrews 13:7, which I left out above, says, "Their work is to watch over your souls, and they are accountable to God." Will you not trust our God to hold them accountable? If the person who is your spiritual leader makes a wrong choice—and they will—God's got that covered. And when you are the person who is a spiritual leader, watch over the souls of those who serve with you.

This would be a really good time to read Gary Molander's chapter on "Covering" from his book *Pursuing Christ. Creating Art.* You can also find it on my Worship Coach blog from April 19, 2014.

INDIVIDUAL CHALLENGE — Set aside some time and pray the words of King David, "Search me, O God...", asking our Father to show you where you struggle with submission. Is it at home? With someone on your team? With someone in leadership at your church? Confess to God. Confess to another believer. Receive forgiveness. Worship gladly.

GROUP CHALLENGE — Break into groups and pray for those who are in authority in your setting, perhaps your worship leader, worship pastor, and lead pastor. Pray for anyone you know who struggles with this submission dynamic of our faith. If you struggle with it, find one person who will commit to help you learn to strengthen this muscle of self leadership.

GOING DEEPER — These resources may serve your journey, especially if you have felt compelled by the Father about a part of your self-leadership that needs to be developed:

*Celebration of Discipline* by Richard Foster

*You're God Is Too Safe* by Mark Buchannon

*Developing the Leader Within* by John Maxwell

*Soul Keeping* by John Ortberg

*Pursuing Christ. Creating Art.* by Gary Molander

*The Artisan Soul* by Erwin McManus

# 3 — LEADING A TEAM

*Care for the flock that God has entrusted to you. Watch over it willingly, not grudgingly—not for what you will get out of it, but because you are eager to serve God.* - 1 Peter 5:2

*Leaders are obsessed with what is best for others, not what is best for themselves.* - Kouzes / Posner

*One of the primary reasons churches are empty is because church leaders love their [ministry] models more than they love people.* - Andy Stanley, Deep & Wide

Team is better.

Doing ministry as a team is slower, stronger, safer, and perhaps most of all, has more significant, longer lasting impact. There is a difference in having a band, a choir, or a ministry... and having a team. You can lead a band that isn't a team. You can lead a choir and not be leading a team. You can even lead a ministry of dozens of people and not have a team.

Teams get things done. Together.

Teams see lives change. Together.

Teams make a difference. Together.

As you might be able to tell by now, I'm a fan of leading as a team.

And to lead a team well, I think there are 5 keys to building that team. We have to do so:

Lovingly

Relationally

Spiritually

Musically

Clearly

## LEAD LOVINGLY

First, you care more about the team member than their gift. If you need a great bass player, and there's a great bass player in your band, you can love that they're a great bass player without loving them. That's not team leadership; that's narcissism. I say that boldly because this has been an area of struggle for me. I wanted great people around me to make me look great. I'm not proud of that, and I'm not fully past it. It's just the truth. But when I started loving people first and their gift second, my leadership effectiveness increased significantly.

Second, you demonstrate your love for them. How do we know God loves us? According to Romans 5:8, "God demonstrates His own love for us in this: While we were still sinners, Christ died for us." (NIV) We know the love God has for us because of what He has done for us. Your team will know the love you have for them when you demonstrate it, not just because you say it. There are a variety of ways to do this, and they are dependent on the person you're loving well, not on you. This is key—we have to know them well to love them well.

If you're familiar with the concept of "Love Languages" from Gary Chapman, start there. He suggests there are 5 ways people give and receive love: Words of Affirmation, Quality Time, Physical Touch, Receiving Gifts, and Acts of Service. In many circles, these have become common lingo. You can simply ask a band, team or choir member —"What's your love language?" Make a note. Put it on your calendar. At least once a month (depending on the size of your ministry, perhaps) find a way to love them in the language they can understand.

> *We have to know them well to love them well.*

If you'd like to go a step deeper, consider this expanded list from the book *Tribal Church*, by Steve Stroope, he breaks down 10 different ways people can feel rewarded, compensated, loved:

- <u>Public Praise</u> - a thank you note might seem meaningless, but hearing their name from you in a rehearsal or service makes them feel appreciated.
- <u>Private Praise</u> - they may not want anyone else to know that you notice, but they want to know that you notice. A "shout out" from the pulpit would make them crawl under the chair, but a word in the hallway would give them a spring in their step.
- <u>Access</u> - if they feel like you're unavailable, they feel like they don't matter. If they feel like you're available to them, they feel valued.
- <u>Input</u> - the opportunity to contribute ideas before major decisions are made. Asking them beforehand means the world to them.
- <u>Added Responsibility</u> - some of us would hate this; we're overwhelmed. Others thrive; we want to have more influence (though not necessarily more tasks).
- <u>Significance</u> - hearing about how what they are doing is making a difference in people's' lives keeps them going.
- <u>Empowerment</u> - having the authority to make decisions concerning their area of ministry without having to get permission feeds their soul.
- <u>Adequate Resources</u> - they want the right music, recordings, and tools to serve at their best.

- <u>Perks or Bonuses</u> - a gift card, lunch on you, gifts, etc. make them feel like they are being rewarded.
- <u>Knowledge</u> - when you suggest a book, a blog, a recording, etc., they feel like you're investing in them. If you give them a resource that is tailored to their role every once in a while, they feel like you are paying them well.

Remember, they won't know you love them because of the feelings in your chest, but by the actions of your hands. This is a part of how you lead a team lovingly.

## LEAD RELATIONALLY

You probably have a couple of friends that you can go for months, even years, without seeing and then just pick up like you'd never been apart. I have four of those guys. I know thousands of people and have led hundreds in ministry. But there are only four that I don't have to stay in touch with to stay connected with. The point? For the vast majority of people you serve, you must stay in touch to lead them well.

It may not be that simple. We need to stay in touch as listeners, not just talkers. This is hard for me. Ask anyone who knows me: I like to talk. So here are some ways I am learning to do better.

a) Text message relationships. About half of the days in any given week I will text the folks in the worship ministry at my church a verse of scripture. On those days when I'm living at a healthy, holy pace, I even pray for each of them when I text them. That's the talking side, as I speak God's word into their lives. (Or at least their phones.) Periodically I will send those same folks a text message asking how I can pray for them. If I'm on a long drive by myself, I'll text before I leave. When I get the text, I pray.

b) Questions. Jesus was a masterful question asker. Next time you're reading in the gospels, pay attention to how amazing He was at that. It really is spectacular. Maybe you and I can learn from Him and ask more questions than we give answers. Again, in an effort to be transparent, I think I've grown from a D- to a C+ in this skill. I am too often too quick to give the answer and too seldom too slow to ask the question. But when we hear other people, we build relationships. Of course this can't be one-sided on their end either. As leaders we typically have a lot to say. This is good. At the right time, in the right way, and especially in a right relationship.

Bottom line? Like boyfriends and girlfriends, husbands and wives, or parents and children, leaders and followers need to spend time together to have a relationship. Learn your team so you can love your team.

## LEAD SPIRITUALLY

When your soul connects with another team member's soul, the team dynamics grow to previously unknown depths. I listed this third in order not because of its importance but because it is a place of inaccessible vulnerability until your team members know you love them, that you are committed to a Godly relationship with them.

Loving spiritually is a context where you disciple one another. Sometimes, because you are the leader, you are the one offering the discipling. Other times, because you are a great question asker, you are the one being discipled. In a relationship characterized by mutual submission, it isn't about who is more in charge or more mature, it is about growing together in Christ.

The way I do this most intentionally is through the lyrics of the songs we're learning and leading. When I ask the band to play a certain way to make much of the text (so that we can make much of Jesus), it stimulates the spiritual side of our relationship. Same with the choir or vocal team, even the tech team. I might ask for a background that really communicates a certain lyric. I sometimes even ask the sound tech to help us punch a moment in a

> *Leading spiritually is a place of inaccessible vulnerability until your team members know you love them, that you are committed to a Godly relationship with them.*

song because of the connection that musical effect has to the text of the song.

Another way we can love spiritually is to pray for each other. Personally. I regularly ask our team members to share requests only about themselves or those in their immediate family. Spiritual connection—soul connection—is made profound when we pray for the deep needs of team members.

Ask your team members for testimonies of God's work in their lives. This creates soul connection throughout the team, but it does something more for you as the leader. Because you are the one asking, it communicates that you expect God to be working in the lives of your team, that you see Him at work, and that you care enough to hear about it. God is at work! Celebrate together and see how this helps you lead them spiritually.

~

CAUTION — this sort of intimacy can lead to an unhealthy attraction and affection between the sexes. It isn't a reason to keep from sharing, but it is a reason to ensure that sharing is done in groups, not pairs. You might also consider breaking into same-gender groups to pray some of the time. If you sense this is a danger zone for your ministry, guard carefully. We have an enemy who is a masquerading as a lion and a master of deception. Manage the tension; don't be naive. Love them enough to protect them.

## LEAD MUSICALLY

Most people on your music team—instrumentalists or vocalists—want to get better. They may not want to go to school to get a degree, so don't treat them like a professor in a classroom. But share with them ways they can excel. If the music they're making is bad, they'll know it, and they won't want to be a team member. If the music they're making is great, they'll know it, and they won't want to miss out on being part of the team.

Learn the culture of your team, your church, and your community. (If you've been there a while, you might need to do a fresh assessment; culture changes rapidly these days.) If there is a low threshold of excellence, go slow, and build a new culture of excellence—based on Biblical teaching. If there is a high threshold for excellence, lean into that, and call them upward. Raise the bar, but don't raise it beyond their ability to reach. When they get there, raise it again. Compliment and challenge. Affirm and advance. Don't flatter and don't exaggerate. Be honest. Love them musically.

## LEAD CLEARLY (EXPECTATIONS AND FEEDBACK)

In my personal experience, unclear and unmet expectations have led to more conflict than anything else in ministry. That's a big statement, and I stand by it. Clarity can serve us so well.

~

My older daughter was a part of a all-star dance team through middle school and high school. They were amazing, and won several national championships. I learned a great deal about coaching and clarity from her dance coach, our friend Andrea. The first thing I learned was that excellence is costly.

With her permission, I've included the list of expectations she sent out when Catherine made the team in Appendix 2. I first read it and thought... "no way parents commit at this level, pay this much money, and follow through with the demands." I was wrong. Andrea's four dance teams now involve over 100 children who pay thousands of dollars and invest hundreds of hours. The result is not just good dancers; it is great teams. Teams that travel all over the country and win. Big.

I wonder if in our grace-filled ministries we've lost sight of the power of excellence. And I wonder if by lowering the standards for excellence in our ministry we have fallen into what German pastor/martyr/author Dietrich Bonhoeffer called *cheap grace*. Jesus came to us full of grace and truth. Full. Of both. Clear expectations don't have to become legalistic.

So how do you clearly communicate what is expected of your teams? In Appendix 3 I have included a document we created soon after I arrived at my church simply called

"Platform Servant Guidelines." I chose the word "guidelines" because I want them to be understood as expectations, not laws. There are times we fail. I am quite sure I don't live up to these guidelines every day, but if we don't have clearly-stated expectations, we will have conflict. That isn't loving people. That is setting them up for pain.

Lead lovingly, relationally, spiritually, musically, and clearly. Your team will be the kind of team others want to be a part of.


INDIVIDUAL CHALLENGE — Set one significant, achievable, measurable goal for yourself in each of these 5 categories. Get them done in the next 5 months, perhaps one each month. Put them on your calendar. Ask someone to check in with you to see how you're doing. At the end of your 5 month challenge, see if you can identify the growth in your team.


GROUP CHALLENGE — Get into groups of 3-5 people and share about the best team experience you were ever part of. It could be a sports team, a music group, or even a church group. Then as a team take 15 minutes to describe an ideal team dynamic in worship ministry. Get back with the large group and share those ideal teams. As time allows, identify 2-3 "next steps" to have that kind of group.

GOING DEEPER — These resources may serve your journey, especially if you have felt compelled by the Father about a part of your team leadership that needs to be developed.

*An Hour on Sunday* by Nancy Beach

*Worship Matters* by Bob Kauflin

*The Five Dysfunctions of a Team* by Patrick Lencioni

*Developing the Leaders Around You* by John Maxwell

*Seven Words of Worship* by Mike Harland and Stan Moser

# 4 — LEADING WITH VISION

*In the last days, God says,*

*I will pour out my Spirit upon all people.*

*Your sons and daughters will prophesy.*

*Your young men will see visions,*

*and your old men will dream dreams.*

Acts 2:17


*Vision without passion is a picture without possibilities... Martin Luther King Jr. did not stand on the steps of the Lincoln Memorial and proclaim, 'I have a plan.' No logical strategy could have inspired people to stand up to oppression or to change the way they treated others. No, with the passion of someone who had suffered prejudice and dreamed of equality, King said, "I have a dream."* - John Maxwell in *Everyone Communicates, Few Connect*


It is easier to have a vision for a program than for a person.

I wonder what it might look like if the vision for your song, service, or ministry morphed into a vision for your people. Maybe this is simply an extension of gifts-based ministry (instead of needs-based ministry). Maybe this is an extension of the parable of the talents (Matthew 25:14-30), where we are charged with investing the "talents" (I love that play on words in the English language) of our people more than creating a moment or an event or an enviable ministry. What if vision for our people drove vision for our ministry?

What if you, ministry leader, were able to sit down with every key leader in your ministry and come up with a shared vision for them spiritually, musically, and relationally? What could that do for the overall vision of the ministry?

For example, what if you had a middle school student that was sensing the call of God on her life to be in worship ministry? What if your songs, services, and ministry were affected by the vision God has for her life? Would that change the way you do what you do? Or how about a college music major that thinks he is ministry bound after graduation? Could it be that instead of "finding a place for him to serve," the fact that God brought him to your church, placed a call on his life, and brought you alongside him might mean the ministry model you have in place needs to be adjusted because of the emerging vision for his life?

I suspect that when we love people well, know them well, and release them to live out their calling, it will significantly shape the songs, services, and ministry we lead. If you aren't the leader of the ministry, perhaps it could still affect the way you serve. Maybe you become more of an encourager and less of a focal point. And if you are that person in middle school or college, maybe you take some initiative to help those around you develop a vision for deployment, where the worship ministry of your team—of your church—becomes a source of worship leaders to serve in church plants, or satellite campuses, or other worship venues on your own campus.

~

Vision can cycle from big to little and back to big again.

John Maxwell offers a great word picture for leadership. He says it's like a motorcycle cop in a funeral processional: The officer starts in front, lights flashing and showing the way. As soon as the group is on the move, she breaks away and goes to the back of the line making sure no one is lost. When the back of the group is moving along, she speeds back to the front to make sure the direction is clear, the destination defined.

Think of your leadership (whether of a song, a service, or a ministry) in similar terms. What is the overall vision, the big picture? Can you articulate it clearly for yourself and those you're leading? Why this song? Why this service plan? Why this season of ministry? But then drill down. Take a song, for example.

"The Power of the Cross" by Keith Getty | Stuart Townend[1]

BIG - This song tells the story of Jesus. It encompasses the gospel. It spans the spectrum from sorrow to celebration. The melody is singable and memorable. The text is rich and powerful.

MIDDLE - The song has 4 verses, each followed by a chorus; the last chorus is slightly different from the first 3. Because the verses tell a story, it is important to include all of them unless there is a compelling reason to leave one out. (Or begin later in the story.) Due to the form of the song, it will help a great deal for each verse to sound different, making the text clear and keeping the worshiper engaged. Consider how many singers on microphone, unison or parts, how many instruments play on each verse, and the dynamics everyone employs.

LITTLE - About halfway through the 3rd verse is a singular moment. The text says "Now the daylight flees; now the ground beneath shakes as its Maker bows His head. Curtain torn in two, dead are raised to life; 'Finished!' the victory cry." At the beginning of that verse, have everyone drop out but piano, perhaps playing up an octave. A single voice on mic. At the word "shakes" have the drummer/percussionist do a drum [1]roll on a low tom or timpani, simulating an earthquake. Have the whole band / team enter softly at "Curtain…" and build dramatically until "Finished!" is sung in triumph. Put that last line on the screen by itself in larger letters. (But not so large as to be hokey.)

MIDDLE - Because of that singular moment—from the "earthquake" to the finished work of Christ on the cross, the song should move toward that moment and away from it. Start the beginning softly, but not so soft as the beginning of that 3rd verse. Make the last verse triumphant, an explosion of celebration. The work of Jesus is finished!

BIG - Prayerfully consider how to come into and out of this song. What could happen musically before and after it, musically and textually? How does it fit in the context of the service?

When considering a song, think from big to middle, then to little and back to big again.

~

The same works with service design.

BIG - Consider a service that is part of a six week series about grace. This particular service is about the joy that comes from living a grace-filled life. What are the things that communicate joy in your context? Light? The music as people enter? The volume of that music? The decor in the room? Color? Do you want to think outside the worship space?

---

[1] Copyright 2005 by Thankyou Music. Administrated by Capitol CMG Publishing

How about at the entrance to the parking lot or the building? Maybe the greeters can give high fives on this particular day instead of handshakes. The whole environment exudes joy.

MIDDLE - What worship elements work during the service to help people connect with the truth of grace-fueled joy? Compile the big pieces:

- sermon
- songs
- videos—purchased or original
- testimonies—live or on video
- readings—ancient or modern "spoken word"
- prayers—written or extemporaneous
- other creative elements that may work in your context: mime, dance, painting, etc.

Consider how you will help those in your congregation who are living in pain come to believe grace and joy can be expressed. Gather more pieces than you have time to put into the puzzle.

LITTLE - Start arranging the pieces of the puzzle. If a song doesn't seem to fit, toss it. If that creative element that seemed perfect in your brainstorming is starting to feel like a square peg in a round hole, set it aside. Craft the way one element leads into the next. If you want to open with "This Is Amazing Grace," then what is the best element to come right after it? Remember the big picture as you think about the "moments" in the service.

MIDDLE - Now that you've gotten into the detail, think about how sections of the service flow. Do you need to add or cut a transition that seemed right earlier in your planning? You couldn't have known that until you got into the detail, but now you do. Plans are made to be changed, so change your plan. By all means, have a Spirit-led plan, but let the Spirit keep leading you as you change it.

BIG - Take a look over the whole experience again. Did digging around in all of that detail strengthen your conviction about a big picture element like the high-five at the door? Or does that now seem trite and out of place? Let the big inform the little and the little affect the big.

~

While it is much harder to describe in a ministry, this "big, middle, little" thinking works at that level too. If the little pieces of your ministry aren't contributing to the overall vision you have for the ministry, then maybe the overall ministry vision needs to be updated. Our church launched a vision to plant 20 churches in less than 20 years. The vision of the worship ministry is clearly to pray for, identify, raise up and equip worship leaders to go plant churches. We teach music lessons. We started a Worship Leader Academy. We developed a strong youth band. We share leadership on the platform in all of our services. Our big vision is to raise up worship leaders to plant churches. That informs the middle vision of involving people. That drives the little vision to the point of mentoring relationships between adult and youth worship leaders. And God is bringing us—from within our fellowship and from outside the walls—worship leaders who will go plant churches.

But if He wasn't, if after years of cultivating this sort of mission in the worship ministry it wasn't happening, we would want to rethink what our role would be in helping the church accomplish her vision. Big to middle to little and back again. How can you use that method to think through your songs, services, and ministry?

INDIVIDUAL CHALLENGE — Customize this for your next step. Are you ready to lead a song, a service, or a ministry? Take time to pray, and when you are aware of God's presence, take 30-60 minutes to walk through the process of big, middle, little, and chart out a song, a service, or a ministry. You don't have to have it finished, but get it started. If you feel like it's ready to roll, take it to someone, and ask about using it.

GROUP CHALLENGE — Do this together. Use what you've learned about teams to craft the design of a song, a service, or a ministry together. Use the creative process to bounce ideas off of one another. Use the process—big, middle, little. When you've finished, celebrate. If possible, find a way to implement your work. Especially if you are crafting a song, see if you can lead it in a service and then debrief together how it worked in real life.

GOING DEEPER — These resources may serve your journey, especially if you have felt compelled by the Father about a part of your vision that needs to be developed.

*An Hour on Sunday* by Nancy Beach

*Visioneering* by Andy Stanley

*Courageous Leadership* by Bill Hybels

# 5 — LEADING BY DESIGN

## THE BIG PICTURE

Have you taken many road trips? I love them. I'm not sure about you, but I prefer a good deal of planning on the front end and a good deal of flexibility in the journey. For example, I like to know that we'll have a place to sleep on a two-day excursion, so I'm inclined to make a hotel reservation just past halfway. I also like to visit favorite spots along the way. On the other hand, I want enough margin to be able to stop and stretch my legs, take a picture, or eat at a new place someone recommends.

Under the guidance and leadership of the Holy Spirit, this mixture of design and flexibility is wise when crafting worship gatherings and service flow. Have a Spirit-led plan. Stay sensitive to the Spirit's promptings during that plan. Make sure you have margin built in—both in terms of time and moment-by-moment spiritual sensitivity—to follow the leading of the Spirit.

If you already have convictions about how to design services, my goal is not to change your mind. Having a conviction and planning by it is more important than which design you use. In fact, I'll share four such structures below. I sometimes carefully follow one of these, and I sometimes intentionally deviate from them. Having a design is essential. Which design you use is optional.

Let the Spirit lead you.

As to leading by design, I have found great effectiveness using one historical and three Biblical models. There are others. For example, Harvest Bible Church in Chicago (Vertical Church Band) has developed a compelling model based on ascending a hill into the presence of God. Bob Kauflin, one my most influential mentors, suggests one in Worship Matters. I haven't tried those yet, but I probably will. Once again: intentionality and thoughtfulness matter more than the model you choose.

~

Exodus 25-27 - The Tabernacle Model

If you've never studied the powerful symbolism in layout of the Tabernacle, I recommend it to you. The care and concern God's nation took in the journey from the Court of the Gentiles to the Most Holy Place was beautiful. In broad strokes, it went something like this:

Outer Courts — Everyone was welcome. There was a strong sense of human interaction: The sounds of the gathered faithful, the sacrifices, songs, and speaking were all overheard but not engaged.

Inner Court — Those who were part of the faith community could actually enter the Tabernacle, the "Tent of Meeting" as it was called. This was not a division based on sinners or holy, but on identity. The people of Israel who entered the tent were aware of their need of forgiveness. They were also aware of Who their God was and that they were His people.

Holy of Holies — Here was the manifest presence of God. It was intimate, holy, and quiet. This is where the law of God was stored. Also in the Ark of the Covenant were reminders of the work of God. The gathered worshipers were keenly aware of The Presence.

~

Psalm 95 - A Common Contemporary Worship Model

The basic shape of this psalm is like a funnel, starting wide open in energy. As you walk through the psalm, the funnel narrows with more moderate energy. At the end, the energy is intimate. No doubt, you have been in worship gatherings that follow this flow: up-tempo and loud, then medium-tempo and powerful (but not as raucous), and finally slow and quiet. Interestingly enough, before the modern worship leader thought of it, David wrote a song like that. Psalm 95:1-7:

> Come, let us sing to the Lord!
>> Let us shout joyfully to the Rock of our salvation.
> Let us come to him with thanksgiving.
>> Let us us sing psalms of praise to him.
> For the Lord is a great God,
>> a great King above all gods.
> He holds in his hands the depths of the earth
>> and the mightiest mountains.
> The sea belongs to him, for he made it.
>> His hands formed the dry land, too.
> Come, let us worship and bow down.
>> Let us kneel before the Lord our Maker,
>> for he is our God.
> We are the people he watches over,
>> the flock under his care.
> If only you would listen to his voice today!

I love the ending of this song, and the simple implications for planning worship. We end the singing portion of the service ready to listen. Close enough to the Father to listen. Aware of the work of Jesus so that our hearts are soft. Sensitive to the Spirit so we can really hear.

Isaiah 6 - A Dialogical Pattern

The pattern in Isaiah 6:1-9 follows this pattern:

- Praise (Holy, Holy, Holy) is directed to God.
- Confession (Woe is me) is offered to God.
- Forgiveness (Your sins are forgiven) is good news from God.
- Word from God (Who will go for us?) is the challenge from God.
- Response from People (Here am I, send me) is the response of the worshiper.

For several years this was my primary model of worship planning. One of its strengths, unlike the Psalm 95 model, is the inclusion of confession and forgiveness. In the modern worship movement, these are often elements of worship that are missing, sometimes for years on end. I'm not convinced this pattern should be followed every time the church gathers, but I again recommend it to you as a beautiful structure through which God's people can journey together.

~

The Four-Fold Pattern of Worship (See Acts 2:42-46)

Bob Webber, long time New Testament professor at Wheaton College, made this pattern common in many pockets of worship renewal. His deep studies into the scriptures and early church history are compelling. The pattern those first Christ-worshipers followed was simple and profound:

- The Gathering - being aware of the faith community and moving into the Presence.
- The Service of the Word - reading scripture, singing scripture, hearing the sermon.
- The Service of the Table - seeing the gospel re-enacted, then experiencing it through touch and taste.
- The Dismissal - being discharged to take the glorious gospel into a world deeply in need.


Entire books have been written on this model, so please forgive my simplification of it. Many of you will see right off how it elevates the Table to be equal with the Word. And many of you may struggle with that. Again, were it not for Dr. Webber's significant research into the New Testament texts and early church writings, I might wrestle with it too. But it seems clear that every time the early followers of Jesus gathered for worship, they broke bread. The death, burial, and resurrection were the hallmarks of the "Followers of the Way," and they reenacted them every chance they got.

Tabernacle, Psalm 95, Isaiah 6, Historical Model... whichever you choose—or another—simply be aware of the magnitude of the task with which you've been entrusted, and trust the God who loves diversity to help you discern the best structure for your services.

## THE MIDDLE PICTURE

Once you have the big picture in mind, move to the middle picture. Primary in most of our minds at this point is probably choosing songs. In order for this to get the full attention it deserves, let me begin by addressing the question: for whom are we choosing songs, or, for whom are we planning worship?

With apologies to Big Daddy Weave (Michael Weaver, singer/songwriter who made popular his great song "Audience of One"), I contend there are three audiences in any worship gathering.

The first audience of Christian worship is our Triune God. This has been an area of great emphasis in recent years. Still, it bears exploration. John 4 is clear: God is seeking worshipers who will worship Him in spirit and in truth. God is the primary audience. When we lose sight of the primacy of this Holy Audience, our gatherings quickly become human-centered, or even idolatrous. Preaching can become so practical that it loses any sense of the transcendent. Testimonies can be so focused on our experiences with God that we never actually experience God—only chasing a previous experience. The singing can use so many personal pronouns that we seek our own emotions over the heart of God, our own ideas over the mind of Christ, and our own stirrings over the Presence of the Spirit. Our first and fullest audience for worship must be Father, Son, and Spirit.

The second audience is the Body of Christ. Consider the broad strokes of the passage in Paul's first letter to the church in Corinth, chapters 12-14. These paragraphs are primarily about the provision of gifts for the purpose of building up the Body—most famously the gifts of faith, hope, and love. Especially key is I Corinthians 14:26: "When you come together, everyone has a hymn, or a word of instruction, a revelation, a tongue or an interpretation. All of these must be done *for the strengthening of the church*." (NIV, emphasis added) Paul was clear—the things we do in worship are for the building up of one another.

The writer of Hebrews describes the same thing a slightly different way. Hebrews 10:21-25 describes the purpose for our encounter with God:

> And since we have a great High Priest who rules over God's house, let us go right into the presence of God with sincere hearts fully trusting him. For our guilty consciences have been sprinkled with Christ's blood to make us clean, and our bodies have been washed with pure water.
>
> Let us hold tightly without wavering to the hope we affirm, for God can be trusted to keep his promise. Let us think of ways to *motivate one another* to acts of love and good works. And let us not neglect our meeting together, as some people do, but *encourage one another*, especially now that the day of his return is drawing near. (emphasis added)

When we neglect meeting together, we don't have the opportunity to motivate one another to do what God has called, equipped, and purposed us to do: acts of love and good works.

Gathered worship has a secondary audience; it is those who have gathered.

There is a third, often ignored or misplaced or unconsidered audience: those who are not yet walking with Jesus. Late in that passage to the Corinthian Christians are some clear instructions about "when an unbeliever" enters the worship gathering. I Corinthians 14:23-25: "...if unbelievers or people who don't understand these things come into your church meeting and hear everyone speaking in an unknown language, they will think you are crazy. But if all of you are prophesying, and unbelievers or people who don't understand these things come into your meeting, they will be convicted of sin and judged by what you say. As they listen, their secret thoughts will be exposed, and they will fall to their knees and worship God, declaring, 'God is truly here among you.'"

Notice how little of what we just explored is for me as I worship, for you as you worship. My worship is designed to glorify God (that's from me), to edify God's people (that's from me), and to testify to those not yet redeemed (that's because of how they see me glorifying God). Yet in our consumeristic culture, God help us, we typically enter a worship gathering thinking about what we receive far more than what we give.

Not only is this weakening our churches, it is weakening our witness.

What does this have to do with song selection? I'd say everything! The content of our songs should glorify God, frequently being directed toward Him. This means lyrics of testimony—while they may glorify the work of our Father— may not fulfill that role. For our worship to be Christian, we have to sing to Jesus, not just sing about God.

> *We typically enter a worship gathering thinking about what we receive far more than what we give.*

How do we strengthen the church? In addition to re-membering together the magnificent Person of Christ, we sing about His redemptive work. We have power for living because the same power that raised Jesus from the dead is ours! (See Ephesians 1:19-20.) There is something physiolog-ical about enunciating the truth of the resurrection that helps us experience the power of it. This infuses us with strength.

Few things are as encouraging, though, as testi-monies. Remember the Samaritan woman who chose to fol-low the teachings of Jesus at the well? When she went back to her village, the whole lot of them were saved on the words of her testimony—before Jesus ever got to the village! (See John 4:39.) There is power in testimony. Revelation 12:11 says we are saved by the blood of the Lamb and the power of testimony. While testimony alone is weak, testimony paired with singing about the greatness of God and the magnificent work of the cross is powerful.

> *They triumphed over him*
> *By the blood of the Lamb*
> *And by the word of their testimony.*
> *Revelation 12:11 (NIV)*

One of the most important things my wife and I can do for our children is love each other well in front of them. They aren't married yet, but they will learn a great deal about how to be married by watching us love one another. The Church is the Bride of Christ. We do a great deal of testifying for the love relationship that is possible for the unbeliever—for those God has created—by loving our Bridegroom well in front of them.

This "indigenous worship" is one of the places where —at least in this time in North American worship—the sounds of our worship gatherings come into play. If you are part of a multi-generational church, it will strengthen each generation differently to sing songs with certain sounds— organ and piano, guitar and drums, choir or vocal team. While we might wish this weren't true, or long for the day it won't be true, it almost certainly is. Do the research. Get to know your people. What strengthens their faith? Do your seniors need to hear "To God Be the Glory" with just the piano every once in awhile? Do your youngest worshipers engage the text better if that electric guitar solo in "How He Loves" (John Mark McMillan / David Crowder) is featured? Do your middle aged adults yearn to hear the songs they grew up with but in a fresh way? Then sing "Blessed Assurance" from Elevation Worship.

If your people aren't engaged, they won't be strengthened. Your job is to find ways to engage them. Their job is to be willing to go on the journey.

## THE LITTLE PICTURE

Once you've gotten to this part it might seem the hard work is done. Maybe. That probably depends on which part of the process you most enjoy. Planning at this level is least fun for me, and therefore the kind of planning I struggle with the most.

You've got the house built—that's the structure/pattern you've chosen. You've got the walls finished—that's the song selection. Now you have to make the flow work from room to room, hanging the decorative pieces that make it all tie together.

And in contemporary worship models, this is usually the most noticeable part. Transitions. How will you start the service (a transition from not engaged to engaged), and then how do you end the first song? What do you do immediately after that? How about between the next two worship elements? Will you say something? Will you or someone play something? If so, what? Often in these places is where we experience dead time. We all hate dead time. It feels awkward. It interrupts the journey. (Nobody likes a flat tire!) That's why it is essential to think through how one element flows into and out of another one. If a non-music person has a role to play, how do they get on stage? When? Does anything happen from the musicians or technicians while they are there?

Attention to detail is often the difference between good and great. When you carefully design the details, your service will make big strides toward great.

Remember, we started this long section by talking about freedom and margin. Don't mistake carefully planning all of these details with inflexibility. Far from it. When you have clear boundaries, it is far easier to feel the freedom to dance in the details. If you've asked the guitar player to play under the pastor's prayer, for example, and then after the prayer you feel compelled to introduce a lyric phrase from the next song, that guitar player can just keep playing. But if that level of detail hadn't been decided ahead of time, that same intro might feel awkward or

> *Plan carefully, and plan with room for the Spirit to lead.*

out of place.

Plan carefully, and plan with room for the Spirit to lead.

INDIVIDUAL CHALLENGE — Pick one of the worship models that is unfamiliar to you, read the corresponding scripture passage, and craft a worship service using that structure. Go into as much detail as you can. If you get stuck, leave out the part you're stuck on, and leave a gap. If you don't know how to fill it when you've finished, ask for help from your pastor, worship pastor, or a friend.

GROUP CHALLENGE #1 — Break into groups and plan a service using as many structures as you have groups. If you have enough for more than five groups, ask one team to come up with a plan not using a model and then share the services with each other. Discuss the potential strengths and weaknesses of each. This will give you a great taste of team worship planning, which can be an absolute blast and have long lasting impact on those who plan as well as those who follow the plan.

GROUP CHALLENGE #2 — Using the same scripture passage and theme, plan a service with the framework of each of the models: Isaiah 6, Historical pattern, Psalm 95, etc.

BONUS CHALLENGE — Take a road trip. You can do this on your own or with a group. (Remember, team is better.) Find 2 or 3 churches within a day-trip distance. Let the worship leader know you're coming and ask them ahead of time if you can have 15 minutes with them. Even better, invite them out for a meal—on you. Then ask questions. Have at least 3-5 open ended questions ready, but after experiencing God together in worship be prepared to ask questions about the worship gathering itself. This can be nearly as effective for your growth as a whole conference, depending on how that conversation goes.

GOING DEEPER — These resources may serve your journey, especially if you have felt compelled by the Father about a part of your vision that needs to be developed.

*An Hour on Sunday* by Nancy Beach

*The Worship Architect* by Constance Cherry

*Handbook for Multi-Sensory Worship* by Kim Miller

*Can We Do That?* by Andy Stanley and Ed Young

# 6 — LEADING WITH MUSIC

*They and their families are all trained in making music before the Lord, and each of them—288 in all—was an accomplished musician.* - 1 Chronicles 25:7

*Faithful stewardship, utilizing to the maximum the gifts each possesses, is the measure of success which should concern a musician in the ministry. The musical talents we have received from God are not exempt from stewardship. The musician is called to give the best he has.* Calvin Johansson in *Music & Ministry*

## PART 1 - THE (UN)IMPORTANCE OF MUSIC

Like all of God's good gifts, music is a wonderful servant but a terrible master. And a horrible idol. Let's admit it: the second most common idol in many churches—after self—is music. Why else would we have experienced "worship wars" over the last half-century? When we make much of music, we make much less of Jesus. When we make much of Jesus, we make less of music. Our Savior didn't say when the music of the church is lifted up He will draw all of mankind to Himself. No, "...the Son of Man must be lifted up, that everyone who believes may have eternal life in him." (John 3-14b-15)

Said another way, music—like the Sabbath—was made for us; we weren't made for music. (See Mark 2:27.) When music stops serving people and people start serving music, we're in trouble.

That said, the most common directive in the Bible is not to love, nor to obey, but to sing. Music is supremely valued by the Author of our sacred texts. And not only singing, but excellence. Reflect on the 33rd Psalm:


Let the godly sing for joy to the Lord;
	it is fitting for the pure to sing to Him.
Praise the Lord with melodies on the lyre;
	make music for him on the ten-stringed harp.
Sing a new song of praise to him;
	play skillfully on the harp, and sing with joy.


I can't imagine playing a ten-stringed harp while singing is an easy skill to master. Excellence is commanded. So there is much to consider about music and its role in worship. In the rest of this chapter, we'll look at choosing the best arrangement of a song, the best key for that song, what context can do for songs, and—for those who need it—a primer on reading music.

## PART 2 - CHOOSING THE BEST ARRANGEMENT (AKA CHART)

In the previous chapter, we talked at some length about choosing songs for worship. Let's take that a littler deeper in this conversation about music. We usually consider a wide variety of things, often without even being aware of it:

Old or new?

Traditional or contemporary?

How traditional, or how contemporary?

Familiar, sort of familiar, or new?

Up tempo, medium, or slow?

Corporate or individual text?

Sung to God, or sung to one another?

We could go on with that list, I imagine, for quite some time. But in this context, I want to approach choosing the right song with a different slant—diving three levels deep.

### First level—Is this the right song?

That's pretty simple, but can be really important. My personal opinion is that the most important song choice is the one right after the sermon, but you could make an argument for the one right before the sermon... or the one that opens the service... or the one that precedes or follows a worship element other than the sermon. For purposes of an illustration, let's decide the right song for a particular slot on a particular Sunday is "In Christ Alone" by Keith Getty and Stuart Townend.[2]

### Second level—Is it the right version of the right song?

In our context, we use sheet music more than chord charts, so my go-to source is PraiseCharts. (More about that in chapter 9.) A quick look at their website reveals there are eight arrangements of "In Christ Alone," some quite different from the others. On the Getty's website there are two very different full orchestrations. On iTunes, there are closer to 100 versions. Great news: Finding the best arrangement is one of the ways we can deeply identify and connect with the heart-song of a local congregation. The more we try different arrangement/styles, the more we can identify what helps connect the hearts of our peopl[2]e with the heart of God.

---

[2] Copyright 2001 by Thankyou Music. Administrated by Capitol CMG Publishing

### Third level—Is there something we can do to customize the best version we can find?

In most of the places I get to lead worship, the arrangement of "In Christ Alone" that seems to work best is by Travis Cottrell on his Alive Forever recording. I tend to be in places that are cross-generational, so the fact that he included the chorus of the old hymn "The Solid Rock" in the middle is meaningful. As I've lived with the text of the song, I've come to a meaningfully different approach to the first part of the third stanza than Cottrell chose. ("There in the ground his body lay, light of the world by darkness slain. Then bursting forth in glorious day, up from the grave he rose again!") This is where I have everyone but the pianist drop out and have her/him play up an octave. At "Then bursting..." the piano returns to where the notes are written and there is a quick two-measure build from *ppp* to *fff* (super quiet to super loud), so the congregation feels the resurrection in the music.

Now, after having sung that particular chart many, many times, it may be time to add another option to the congregation's library. I'm leaning toward the one from the Passion movement by Kristian Stanfill.

The specifics are less important here; your choices should be highly contextualized. What works in the region, town, neighborhood, or church you are in? The right customization of the right arrangement of the right song can change from church to church or year to year, so keep learning from the people you are leading with and leading for. Make sure you lead with the very best music for those people.

## PART 3 - CHOOSING THE BEST KEY

From the original recording or print music, you can change keys up or down. There are many reasons people choose to do this. If the song is too high or low for the leader, for example. Or if the guitar player can only play in certain keys. Or if you want to use middle school students to play in a church orchestra. (Hint: don't use B major; it will be utterly unknown to them at that stage of development.) School bands usually start with the key of Bb, then F, then other keys with flats. Then sharps.

When you change the key of a song, several things are affected. The guitar player is probably the most impacted member in the rhythm section. In general, the more sharps or flats, the more difficult. Guitar players seem to prefer keys that include sharps. Pianists tend to prefer flats.

As a worship leader, your primary reason to choose a key should be to make it possible for the people you're leading to sing. Most congregations can comfortably sing about a dozen notes: A, B, C, D, E, F, G, A, B, C, D, E and maybe (but not at the early service) F. That's comfortably. Many, many recorded modern worship songs go up to a G. Changing the key may be the best way to serve those you lead.

Of course we sing different songs, well, differently. So when you want them to sing quietly and reflectively, the song should be in the lower part of their voices. Conversely, when you want them to really belt it out, the song should be in the upper part of the congregational range. Most importantly, pick the key of a song because of the congregation, not the leader.

Also worth knowing—the more flats, the warmer the sound. Darker. The more sharps, the brighter the sound. Happier. So the change from B to Bb isn't just a half step down and better for pianists than guitars; it changes the characteristics of the sound from very bright to a little warm.

Conventional wisdom is not to change they key more than 2 steps up/down from the original. Since choosing a key is primarily for the benefit of those we lead, this guideline may mean you use different leaders for different songs. Bottom line? Make it about serving the congregation, not the leader.

## PART 4 LEADING IN CONTEXT — Biblical, Historical, Narrative

Music never exists in a vacuum. Associations are powerful. Consider these three stories from history.

1) Martin Luther, the infamous reformer, was for the people. He wanted the people to have access to the scriptures. That wasn't normal in the early 1500s. He wanted people to sing. All people. And so when walking by a sa-

loon, he heard a drinking song. Legend has it that he went back to his little room and wrote "A Mighty Fortress," a powerful poem that is set to that drinking song. Luther famously asked the question, "Why should the devil have all the good music?"

2) On the flip-side, for a long time after World War II, it was difficult for many people in the United States to sing "Glorious Things of Thee Are Spoken" because the tune used in most hymnals was the same melody to which the Nazis sang the German national anthem (AUSTRIA). I remember Wayne Johnson, my college music professor, sharing with us that it took him decades to get past that association.

3) Early in the contemporary Christmas music era—the late 1970s and 1980s—there were thousands of churches that associated the sound of drums with the sound of rock-n-roll, thereby choosing to resist newer forms of music. In fact, there was an entire book written on the subject. This is a compelling reason to have (and teach) a healthy understanding of the theology of sacred and secular. The Bible doesn't seem to make this distinction like many people in our time. The testimony of scripture seems to be that if it is part of God's creation, it is good. (See 1 Timothy 4:4-5 and 1 Corinthians 10:31.) Sounds, rhythms, and instruments are all morally neutral.

## PART 5 — WHAT WE REALLY NEED TO KONW TO READ MUSIC

If you have a music degree (or two or three), you might want to skim over the rest of this chapter. Chances are you don't need to learn "real world music theory" I've shared. However, if you are going through this with your team—and I hope you will—it may serve your process to explore it together. When I taught this to my first group of Worship Leader Academy students, I was surprised at how interested they were. Their level of interest is why I trust you may want to learn too.

Here's the scoop: I spent years in high school, college, and seminary learning how to read music. Eventually I figured out most of what these brilliant professors were teaching me. To be honest, I actually liked most of it; that's just one of the many ways I'm weird. But as a practitioner in a modern church, I probably need to know about 20% of what they so faithfully taught me. Then again, there are a few things they didn't teach me that have become important to know.

Before I offend any music professors out there too deeply, let me say: I don't think it was wasted energy. I am a better musician because of how deeply we drilled down into the theory of music. In general terms, I think those things serve me every day. But if I just boil down what I really need to know to lead a band, or even a choir—the basics—then I'd call that…

## Real world music theory

For example, here are a list of things that serve me nearly every rehearsal:

- Being able to tell what key a song is in
- Knowing what time signature a song is in
- Easily following the "road map" of a song
- The basic form of a song
- Tuning - flat and sharp
- Basic chord progressions
- Major chords, minor chords, and 7ths
- Rhythmic notation — especially for vocalists/choirs
- What a measure is
- What an accidental does
- Common music terms

On the other hand, here are some things I've not thought about since graduation:

- The names of cadences (masculine, feminine, etc.)
- The church modes (Dorian, Phrygian, Mixolydian, etc.)
- Bizarre time signatures (like 1/1 or 10/8)
- All the names for various forms of songs (Bar form, Rondo, etc.)

And here are some things I wish I'd learned at least a little bit about:

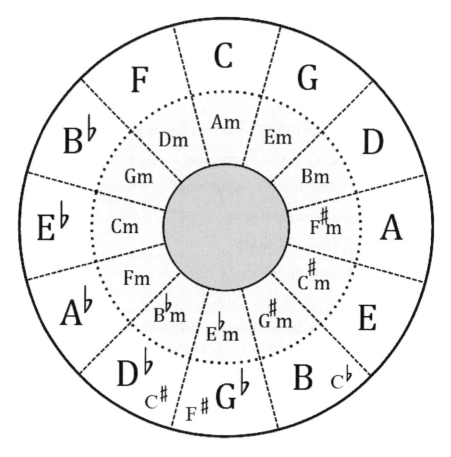

- The Nashville number system
- Tablature (for guitars)
- Transposition basics, especially for guitar/capo
- Slash notes and why they matter (bass guitar, piano, guitar)
- How the voicing of chords affects sound on piano and guitar

So let's dive into real world music theory. Just the basics. (For a glossary of common musical terms, see Appendix 4.)

**What key is this song in?**

The easiest way to tell what key a song is in is probably deciphering the key signature. There is a trick used in music theory to help with this called a "Circle of Fifths." If you like visual aids, this is super helpful. If you prefer memorization, just look over the list and memorize. I'll include both for you here:

No sharps, no flats - C major (or A minor)

One sharp - G major (or E minor)

Two sharps - D major (or B minor)

Three sharps - A major (or F# minor)

Four sharps - E major (or C# minor)

Five sharps - B (or G# minor)

Six sharps - pick a different key! (Actually it's F# major and 7 sharps is C# major, but those songs are nearly unheard of.)

One flat - F major (or D minor)

Two flats - Bb major (or G minor)

Three flats - Eb major (or C minor)

Four flats - Ab major (or F minor)

Five flats - Db major (or Bb minor)

Six flats - Gb major (or Eb minor)

Seven flats - strangle the composer (No, don't. That's Cb and exceedingly rare.)

**What time signature is this song in?**

There are two broad categories when it comes to metering time: 2 and 3. Every song I've heard done in church is in sets of 2 or sets of 3.

The two most common time signatures are 4/4 and 3/4 — 2 sets of 2 or 1 set of 3. Chris Tomlin's "Amazing Grace; My Chains Are Gone" is in 4/4; the original hymn tune is in 3/4. Listen to or look at the music to hear the difference.

Simply put, the top (or first) number is how many beats in a measure—and whether it is a group of 2 or 3; the bottom number is what kind of note gets the beat.

2/4 = 2 quarter notes in a measure (feels like 2)

3/4 = 3 quarter notes in a measure (feels like 3)

4/4 = 4 quarter notes in a measure (feels like 2+2)

6/8 = 6 eighth notes in a measure (feels like 2 groups of 3)

9/8 = 9 eighth notes in a measure (feels like 3 groups of 3)

12/8 = 12 eighth notes in a measure (feels like 4 groups of 3)

**How can I follow the road map of this song?**

This road map thing seems to trip up most of my choir members who don't claim to be music readers... and some who do. These symbols are your friends when deciphering the map of music:

If you see the first one of those symbols, then sooner than later the second will appear. It could be in a 1st ending or just all by itself. Whenever you see that second symbol, look for its mirror image, and start there a second time. If it is in a first ending, the the second time you sing/play that part take the 2nd ending. This one piece of information is probably 40% of what you need to know to follow music!

The rest of the terms are a little more, well, Italian:

• D.C. - the beginning (Da capo literally means "the head")
  • When you see D.C. in the music, simply go back to the beginning of the song.
• D.S. - the sign (Del Signo or "from the sign")

- When you see D.S. in your music, go back to where you see this symbol: 𝄋
- Coda - tagged on to the end (literally means "tail")
  - When you see this symbol ⊕, go to the last part of the song; it will be marked "Coda."

When you're learning a piece of music at home, simply go through and circle or highlight those on your sheet music (or Music Stand app) and follow the instructions. It usually isn't hard once you crack the code. If you get stuck, ask a friend more experienced with reading music for help.

**The basic form of a song**

Intro, V, Ch, Br, Tag = Intro, Verse, Chorus, Bridge, and Tag
When leading a rehearsal, it is helpful to know about basic terms such as intro, verse, chorus, bridge, and tag (or coda). Verses (V) tend to be the same or very similar musically but different textually. Choruses (Ch) are nearly identical in both music and text. Bridges (Br) are new material, different from both verse and chorus. They usually follow a chorus and lead back into a verse (V) or chorus (Ch). Bridges are often repeated. The intro is what the instrument(s) play before anyone sings. The tag is how the song ends—often including a shortened part of the chorus. These are all flexible, which is part of what keeps songs sounding different from

one another. In general, those are the big chunks found in most songs.

These days the most common form tends to be something like:

Intro, V, Ch, V2, Ch, Br, Br, Br, Ch, Tag

Of course, there are lots of variations. Here's why this is so helpful—in that common form (which may not be so common by the time you're reading this) if you learn the chorus and bridge—just two sections—you actually know more than half the song. Learn the verse and you're up to nearly the whole thing. It makes learning much faster when you look at the big picture.

## Accidentals should be on purpose

When you see something like a squashed b next to a note, (e.g. ♭) it lowers it a half step. When you see what look like a number sign (e.g. ♯) next to a note, it raises it a half step. When you see an awkward symbol that doesn't look familiar (e.g. ♮) it cancels out a flat or sharp, making the note natural. These are helpful concepts—flat, sharp, and natural—because they cross over in the language of singing or playing in tune.

## Tuning - flat and sharp

With inexpensive electronic tuners (yes, there's an app for that), this is less of a human skill than it used to be. But even when you start a song or service all tuned up, strings stretch, humidity in the room changes, and it is important to be able to hear if a note is sounding too high (sharp) or too low (flat) so you can self-correct. If you're leading and someone is singing or playing out of tune, it is far more helpful to be able to say to them (with grace and gentleness), "I think you're a little flat" on that note/section/song. Or, "You may be over singing because you sound a little sharp to me." (Maybe this is a good time to go back and read the section on leading lovingly.)

## Basic chord progressions

If you are an instrumentalist, you already know how helpful this is. When you can predict with 90% accuracy what the next chord is going to be, it can save impending crash after impending crash. As thankful as I am for the 10% that gives such creativity, diversity, and beauty to music, I'm thankful that most of the time there is a familiarity that comes with predictability. Knowing these predictable patterns helps develop skill for just about all instrumentalists. The muscle memory you learn going from D to Am to C to G in "Revelation Song" comes in very handy when those same chords appear in the same order, even if the strum pattern, tempo, or groove is different. Familiarity with predictable chord progressions can streamline your learning.

## Major chords, minor chords, and 7ths

When I was a kid, I remember hearing, "If the chord sounds happy, it's major. If it sounds sad, it's minor." That's still pretty accurate, but if you can identify and think of chords as major or minor, it cuts down on the chance of playing the wrong chord. This is a place where you can go a little deeper and benefit a lot more, but since we're sticking with the basics—real world music theory—I'll leave that up to your further study. (e.g. Which chords are major and minor in which keys?)

## Rhythmic notation — especially for vocalists/choirs

If you're reading a chord chart, you will never have to know what rhythm looks like on a page. If you are a singer, or if you are in a choir that uses sheet music, it will speed up your learning curve to know a little bit about rhythm. At a very basic level: the less weighed down a note is the longer it lasts. A whole note, which gets four beats—a whole measure in 4/4 time—is just an empty circle. A sixteenth note, which only gets 1/4th of one beat, is a filled-in note with two flags on a stem. Add more stuff to a note, and it goes faster. Here are the most common notes:

| | | | |
|---|---|---|---|
| 𝅝 | = whole note | 𝅗𝅥. | = dotted half note |
| 𝅗𝅥 | = half note | ♩ | = quarter note |
| ♪ | = eighth note | ♪ | = sixteenth note |
| ▬ | whole rest | ▬ | half rest |
| 𝄽 | = quarter rest | 𝄾 | = eighth rest |

## What's a Capo (do)?

A capo is only really useful on an acoustic guitar. By placing the capo on the neck of the guitar, you raise the sound of the key 1/2 step. If the song is in Eb, and the guitar player plays in D but puts the capo on the first fret, it will sound in Eb, up one half step. This is a great tool for changing the sound roughly the same amount as you would change the key of a song—two whole steps or four half steps. The resulting capo placement is no higher than the 5th fret. Advanced guitar players will use their capo for other things, like making it possible for them to play certain chords in certain voicing or to make the sound of the guitar brighter—almost mandolin like. Some will tune down the guitar and use a capo. The best way to learn more is to ask questions of a knowledgeable guitar player in your circle of friends.

~

The better we connect our music to the truths of scripture, the more authority we gain. For example, do we want to use a quiet, meditative piece in a church that is more comfortable with "getting through the music" so we can hear the sermon? Introduce it with Psalm 46:10, "Be still and know that I am God" or "The Lord is in his holy temple. Let all the earth keep silence before him." (Habakkuk 2:20) Perhaps in your context, you are confronted by people who think there's too much commotion or too much noise in your gatherings. Read Psalm 150 or Revelation 5:11 where we learn just how epic the sounds of heaven were revealed to John:

> *"Then I looked again and I heard the voices of thousands and millions of angels around the throne and of the living beings and the elders. And they sang in a mighty chorus: 'Worthy is the Lamb who was slaughtered—to receive power and riches and wisdom and strength and honor and glory and blessing.'"*

I can't imagine how massive the sound of millions of angels must be. Can you?

INDIVIDUAL CHALLENGE — Choose 2-3 areas of "Real World Music Theory" that aren't easy for you, and dive in.

GROUP CHALLENGE — Quiz each other. See if you can find little tricks to share with one another. Feeling extra ambitious? Create a game that each team / group plays, perhaps something like a "Real World Music Theory" version of Pictionary.

# 7 — LEADING WITH TECHNOLOGY

Let me be honest: I am not a trained audio, video, or graphic artist. I have more to learn than I do to offer. Still, having thought through these roles for years, I think I can offer some perspective that will be helpful to you who are technical artists as well as those of you who will be serving alongside and leading those servants.

From that perspective, here are a few general comments about production teams and then a bit about each role.

These brothers and sisters are part of the worship team. They should be appreciated, communicated with, included, and valued just as much as the finest singers or instrumentalists in the ministry. While they are responsible for serving those on the platform, it is considerate for those on the platform to regularly ask those in the booth if they need anything. We serve one another. We submit to one another. We love one another.

Production teams need to be discipled just like platform teams do. It might work differently; tech-oriented folks tend to have different personalities. Nevertheless, it is essential for the worship ministry to find ways to help these servants grow in their likeness to Jesus. Just because we don't see them model worship on a stage doesn't mean they should worship with any less depth. Just because they aren't using a microphone to share what they are learning about their faith doesn't mean they shouldn't be learning in their faith. When the team prays after a rehearsal, invite them to join you. When the team prays before services, invite the production team to join you. When you share insights to lyrics, to scripture, to faith—include this team. They are part of leading worship. They need to grow in Christ just like everyone else does.

~

If you're on the production team, the greatest power you for leading the congregation lies in paying attention. Keep your eyes up. (I know of churches that have these servants put their phones in a basket until the service is over so they won't be distracted.) Think ahead so you're never behind. In my experience, at least nine of ten mistakes made in the tech ministry, maybe even 99 of 100, happen because someone wasn't paying attention. Something so simple, yet so difficult—and it can make all the difference.

## SOUND

- The congregation needs to hear the spoken word, whether over top of music or without it.
- The congregation needs to hear the melody: words and notes.
- The platform personnel need a decent monitor mix.

Everything beyond these three core concepts is for the realm of audio engineers. The better everything else gets, the better the worship gathering will be. If anything gets in the way of these, including a spectacularly equalized guitar or perfectly mic'd choir, or having a picture perfect gain structure across the sound board—as beautiful as those things are —they still come second to these big three.

I find it fascinating, having worked with dozens of sound techs over more than 30 years, how deeply those servants value the sweet mix that just clicks. I love it too! Strive for excellence here. Strive for excellence everywhere. For at least 95% of those in the gathering—maybe more—it just doesn't matter. Don't get me wrong. I'm glad it matters to sound techs. It should. It matters to me. But if the perfect mix gets in the way of hearing the melody, the spoken word, or the monitor mix, the cost is too high.

It is a matter of attitude and priority. Audio artists serve the folks in the crowd and those on the platform. They don't serve the mix; they serve the people. It's sort of a "sabbath was made for man, not man for the sabbath" thing. (Mark 2:27.) The experience of the people is highest priority.

Nearly every sound person I've served with—for a single service/event or for years—has gotten this right. It is beautiful. They are among the most servant-hearted, servant-minded people I've ever known. They work harder than anyone knows. They spend hours and hours doing thankless, lonely work. They are a treasure when their attitudes are like those described in Ephesians 5:21, "submitting to one another out of reverence for Christ."

## VIDEO (GRAPHICS)

- The presser of the space bar has become the leader of the congregation.
- The lyrics must be accurate and clear, and they should look good.
- The backgrounds should serve the lyrics, not just the eyes of the content designer.

More focus is required from the person operating the computer than anyone on the team. One slip during a song and the majority of the congregation is interrupted. That's a lot of pressure. So here are a couple of tips for who you ask to serve in this role...

A. Know the songs. It helps if this person has some musical skill. The timing is so important that knowing how music works can help immensely. The best video folks I've worked with know music and they know the songs really well.

B. Don't choose someone who struggles with ADD or ADHD. Even if it isn't an official diagnosis but they tend to be a bit scattered, find a different place for those folks to serve.

C. Accuracy is more important than artistry. That may not be true at every position in a worship ministry, but it is here. The wrong background is not good. Failure to advance the screen is terrible. (Well, relatively speaking.)

In order for the lyrics to be accurate, develop and follow a style sheet when it comes to capitalization, punctuation, and line breaks/page breaks. The right words, in the right order, in the right format. These are beautiful things, even in their simplicity.

My preference is to use a poetic layout—capitalize first words on each line, names and pronouns for God (and other proper nouns, if applicable), and first words of new sentences. If you're using IMAG (image magnification) then two lines of text on the bottom third is plenty. If you're using images or motion backgrounds, four lines of text is ideal. Five is okay. Six is usually too many. Because the poetry is being sung, there may be times when the line break looks a little odd in order to make it easy to sing.

Examples of "not so good" and "pretty nice" are pictured here for a challenging song to get just right. Sing along with David Crowder's "Come and Listen"[3] and see if this helps:[3]

Times New Roman has seraphs.

[3] Copyright 2005 by sixsteps Music, worshiptogether.com songs. Administrated by Capitol CMG Publishing

Text is overwhelmingly big.

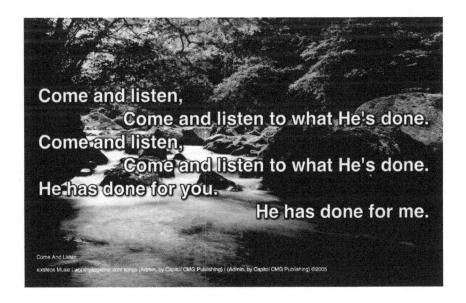

Text layout is hard to follow.

He has done for you.
He has done for us.
Come and listen,
Come and listen to what He's
done.
Come and listen,
Come and listen to what He's
done.

Lines of text awkwardly wrap.

Come and listen,
Come to the water's edge all you
Who know and fear the Lord.
Come and listen,
Come to the water's edge all you
Who are thirsty come.
Let me tell you what He
Has done for me.
Let me tell you what He
Has done for me.

Too many lines of text.

Those are things to avoid. On the other hand, here is what we have found to serve the text, the people, and the artistic eye:

For most churches, the font should be 4"-5" on the screen, so allow that to determine the style and size you set at the computer. Fonts that don't have serifs are typically easier to read. If you're using HD this is probably not an issue. If you're not yet in HD, make sure there is adequate shadow and/or outline to be able to see the font clearly over what is behind it. Oversized and over bolded fonts look hokey. Remember, one of the audiences in our worship services are the not-yet-redeemed. What they see should be visually appealing.

Use creative leadership here. Songs have a vibe, a feel. Good songs ensure that this vibe is an extension of the lyrics. If not using IMAG, the backgrounds chosen for songs should match the vibe. Our goal is to make much of Jesus by making much of the text. Backgrounds can either support that or oppose it. A little intentionality can go a long way in pursuit of this goal.

## LIGHTS

- There is a tension to manage between anonymity and community with house lights.
- The use of color is powerful and should serve the lyrics.
- The potential for distraction is great, as is the potential for focus. Err on the side of focus.

Guests often like to feel anonymous. Younger people are typically more comfortable with a darker worship space. Long time members of a church want to see their friends across the room. Older generations are typically uncomfortable in a worship space that is very dark. Darker house light increases anonymity and diminishes community. Brighter house light has the inverse effect. For many, dark equates with watching a show on the platform, and light equates participating with those on stage.

Manage the tension.

Learn your congregation; then, lead them well. Where I serve, the tension needs to be on the side of community, but they'd be very comfortable with moments that are darker. This reflects the church I'm in. The last church I served? Quite a bit darker in the blended service and very dark in the contemporary service. It fit that church. Know your people, and manage the tension.

Color is beautiful and powerful. Artists have known this for centuries. God knew it when he thought of sunrises and sunsets. Romantics know the beauty of candlelight dinners. Just like background choices for the screens, lighting choices should serve the vibe of the song so they both serves the vibe of the text. Integrating colors from backgrounds into a lighting scheme can bring beauty and power to the worship environment.

Because lighting is so powerful, it should be used wisely. With good lighting design, you can have a whole room suspend reality and focus on a single person, scene, or worship element. With bad lighting design, you can make a whole room distracted, confused, even anxious. Learn your people. Learn your craft. You can have massive impact by unleashing the power of Biblical truth through the wise use of lighting.

## CONCLUSION

As you might gather by now, everything emerges from the Biblical text: the sermon, the song lyrics, the sounds to make the most of the song lyrics, the backgrounds to make the most of the song lyrics, integrated lighting to make the most of the backgrounds to make the most of the song lyrics, the audio mix to make the most of the sounds that make the most of the song lyrics, and the personnel who can make the most of the song lyrics. ALL of this should be able to trace its way back to the scriptures. In other words, if the background of the slide is blue, and there's a color wash on the back wall that's blue, there's a way to trace that to the scripture for the sermon for the day. We aren't making much of the sermon; we're making much of the scripture—and ultimately not just the words of God but the Word of God, Jesus Christ.

## One More Word for Technical Artists

My technically-minded brothers and sisters, I implore you: please do not hide in the tech booth. Serving Jesus can be a breakthrough way to grow in your faith. For many of us, it is. But serving Jesus in the relative isolation of the booth—and with the honorable goal of not being noticed—can trigger a desire to be left alone spiritually and relationally. Here's the thing: you are still part of the body of Christ. The words of 1 Corinthians 12:14-15 say, "The body has many parts, not just one part. If the foot says, 'I am not a part of the body because I am not a hand,' that does not make it any less a part of the body." We could safely reword that to read: Your church has many people, not just one person. If the technician says, "I am not part of the faith community because I am in the booth," that does not make them any less in need of spiritual intimacy. As much as serving can unlock greater growth, it is not a substitute for transformative community. Please don't hide. Your church needs you to grow in Christ. You need to, too. It's God's plan for your life.

INDIVIDUAL CHALLENGE — Spend an hour with someone on the other side of the worship team—platform or tech. Ask what it is like, especially when it comes to the partnership between platform and booth. Talk about how that relationship can be strengthened in your ministry.

GROUP CHALLENGE — If possible, use 30 minutes of a "bonus rehearsal" to swap roles: ten minutes of orientation, ten minutes of making music, and ten minutes to debrief. Talk about the things that surprised you in that 30 minute experience.

GOING DEEPER

*Guide to Sound Systems for Worship* by Jon Eiche.

## 8 — LEADING GREAT REHEARSALS

Are you just getting started?

The best way to learn to lead great rehearsals is to start leading rehearsals. (Thank you, Captain Obvious!) But wait, there's more! After the rehearsal, ask for feedback. Make note of three things you would do differently. Then run them by a more experienced member of your group. Ask for one or two additional suggestions from them. Before you do that, here are a few things that might help you start well.

### HAVE A PLAN

#### BEFORE

What do you want the room to be like when people come in? Do you want music playing that will be rehearsed? Want it bright and loud? Or normal? Or subdued and quiet? That probably depends on your first song.

## BEGINNING

Start with something familiar and energetic. It doesn't have to be the most familiar or the most energetic, but much like a worship gathering something that communicates joy is a great way to start. Don't work too much on this familiar song, but also don't let familiarity turn into auto-pilot singing and playing. You can use these opening ten minutes or so to remind the rhythm players to tighten up. You can remind vocalists to give attention to words, looking for key concepts—even to uncover a deeper meaning in a turn of phrase. Consider it a warm up for voices, fingers, ears, mind, heart, and spirit. Regularly in our rehearsals, I will challenge our folks to move beyond practicing music to practicing worship.

I've also discovered that it helps us get rolling if we start making music right away, otherwise people are still setting up, tuning, tweaking stuff. When we start making music, we are all on the right page as quickly as possible. After the opening song, you can check the monitor mix, re-tune a guitar, etc.

## MIDDLE

After the opening song, tackle either the new song or the one that needs the most work. This is the song that will take the longest, and you'll have their best attention and energy during this part of the rehearsal. Celebrate little victories along the way with the new song. Encourage, encourage, encourage. Your team wants to do well; they usually want to please the leader. So when you encourage, you bolster their efforts and reward their hard work.

After the hard song, do something to recover. A simple song. Something different might be refreshing, but something similar might be easier. You have a lot of freedom here. See what works with your group. Not everyone responds the same way to hard work. If your singers are vocally tired, do a little more work with the band, or do something easy to sing.

Once you are satisfied with the individual songs, turn your attention to transitions. Make sure to leave time to address this. Transitions are harder to make effortless; they often feel awkward. They need lots of time and attention.

## ENDING

You can effectively end rehearsal in a couple of ways: with a song easy to do well, or repeat the hard / new song. The most important thing about the last song is that it helps your team leave feeling like winners. Every time I break this rule, I hate the end of rehearsal. It stays with me all night and sometimes through the next day. Every time I follow this rule, I leave energized and motivated. Perhaps you've had this same experience, whether as leader or participant in a rehearsal.

So, start with upbeat and familiar, move to new and / or hard, rebound with easy, hit the transitions, and end with victory. Hopefully that gives you lots of freedom and a helpful outline.

~

> *Have as much of a plan for discipleship as you do for music.*

What about prayer or devotional time? Again, what's most important is to think about it, and do it on purpose. You could open and close with prayer. You could open or close with prayer. You could break in the middle, maybe after the new song. I tend to let the lyrics of the songs drive the devotional part of rehearsal. You could do a slow walk through a book study using *The Heart of the Artist* by Rory Noland, *Worship Matters* by Bob Kauflin, or a favorite of your own. Your team and your approach should serve your context. The core takeaway: Have as much of a plan for discipleship as you do for music.

## AFTER

Remember, you're rehearsing people, not music. Use the time after rehearsal to visit with folks on the team.

Whenever possible, plan to linger for at least 15-20 minutes. You don't want to keep those who need to move on, but you do want to be available to those who need to talk. Or pray. Or seek counsel—musical, spiritual or relational. The moments after rehearsals can be among the most potent in an entire week.

## BE PREPARED

There are at least three ways it is important for you to walk into the rehearsal prepared: spiritually focused, musically clear, and logistically organized.

**Spiritually focused.** Are you "prayed up?" Are you aware of the lyric content—including how they connect to scripture? Have you considered ways to demonstrate how deeply you are for the people on your team? This doesn't necessarily require a great deal of time, but it does take at least a few minutes in close proximity to the rehearsal. Pray for each team member by name. Think of a way to encourage them. (Go back and skim over the chapter on leading a team.) Look over the texts of the songs. Remember what motivated you to choose them to lead your church family in the first place.

**Musically clear.** This involves several elements. Let's start with form. Do you have a plan for what order to do the song in—verses, choruses, and bridges? Will you do it just like the print music or a recording? Which recording? Do you want to start with the chorus? Or end with a drop chorus? Know this ahead of time. If possible, communicate it ahead of time. But be open to the life of a song in rehearsal, too. You may discover that someone on the team has a great idea to make the song more fun, more powerful, or more tender.

It is also imperative that you know when you want instruments to play or not play and singers to sing or not sing. Want to start with just guitar, add bass, then have keys and drums join? Or is everyone in at the beginning? How will you differentiate among the verses, the chorus, and the bridge? If you're doing two choruses in a row, how will you make the second one different? Who will lead out vocally? If it is a female, when do you want to guy harmony to kick in? Think through this before the rehearsal so you have a clear vision of the song. It is impossible to get a band (or choir) to sound like your preferred vision if you can't first imagine and articulate that vision. Make sure these decisions make much of the text so you and your team can make much of Jesus.

**Logistically organized.** The biggest time drain I see when less experienced folks take lead in a rehearsal is a lack of logistical organization. This includes things like having music copied, equipment properly placed and hooked up, and microphones and instruments line-tested. I've seen 30 minutes of a 60-minute rehearsal spent on addressing these issues. Clearly communicate to your team so they know how to start. Are they supposed to bring their own printed music or iPad? Is the sound technician aware of the stage set up, and do they know they are to hook everything up and line test it at least 15 minutes before the rehearsal? Lean into your team. Leaders are repeaters. You may need to communicate these shared expectations every few weeks or months.

One more thought: Consider how much you will dictate these things and how much you will invite participation. You may have such a clear vision for a song or a set or a service that you don't really need the drummer tossing out suggestions. If that's the case, let your folks know ahead of time. Develop that as your rehearsal culture. I tend to invite lots of suggestions from my teams. Typically, they have better ideas than I do, and if they didn't have the freedom to speak up, we would never be as good as we are. Again, clearly communicate this dynamic to your team. If you want input, ask for it. If you ask for it, be prepared to use it. Or at least try it.

~

INDIVIDUAL CHALLENGE — Put together a mock rehearsal plan for this past Sunday's service, especially making note of anything you wish had been done differently.

GROUP CHALLENGE — Exchange your mock rehearsal plan with one another then identify five positive things, and offer two suggestions or ideas for improvement. Another option would be to collaborate: Come up with at least 10 different options for how to approach devotional time in rehearsals.

BONUS CHALLENGE — Take another road trip. The questions may be different now, and if you're doing this as a group, the interaction will be too. By now you may have learned different things to look for, listen for, and pay attention to. Think carefully about ideas you can take home. Not everything another church does is something you should do, of course. But we can all learn from one another. Road trips are one of our favorite ways to learn!

GOING DEEPER — These resources may serve your journey, especially if you have felt compelled by the Father about a part of your self-leadership that needs to be developed:

*Worship Matters* by Bob Kauflin
*An Hour on Sunday* by Nancy Beach

# 9 — LEADERSHIP RESOURCES

There has never been a day in history with as many worship resources as there are today. A massive library of historical hymns and songs have passed the test of time. An unparalleled number of modern songs are being written and shared every year. I just entered the theme "worship" on the Christian Copyright License Incorporated (CCLI) SongSelect website. There were 11,524 songs that came up. When I tried "praise," it returned 18,529 songs.

The problem isn't so much finding resources as sorting through the myriad of resources to get to the right ones for you and your church. I hope these thoughts and lists can help.

~

First, let's not overlook the most powerful resource available: The Bible. You may have immediately flashed to the Psalms, the hymnal Jesus sang from. But there are many other songs in the pages of scripture, too. There are prayers, admonitions, and stories. One phrase from a scripture passage spoken between verses of a song can refocus the congregation on God.

When there is an instrumental interlude in a song, I frequently put a verse of scripture connected to the truth we're singing on the screen. This connects Biblical authority with experiential participation and helps worshipers connect the dots. For example, project Psalm 103:1 during "10,000 Reasons" or Revelation 4:8b-11 during "We Fall Down."

We use scripture at other times too. There are some times we'll use a short passage as a Call to Worship. We regularly use Biblical benedictions in lieu of closing prayers. (Among our favorites are Numbers 6:24-26, Ephesians 3:17-21, Hebrews 13:20-21, and Jude 24-25.)

The next resource most of us think about is music. Songs. Let me offer this preface to where to find songs: As you find lyrics that connect the hearts of those in your congregation with the heart of God, pay attention to where they come from so that, in turn, you can more easily find similar songs that are more likely to help those you lead engage with God. A word of caution though, don't let this overly confine your musical variety. At least a few times a year, try a song from a different stream of contemporary music.

Below are ten different sources of contemporary worship music. Since the songs are (somewhat) contemporary to the time of this writing, it will be out of date sooner than later. Still, the concept holds. So pay attention to writers, ministries, or labels that seem to be effective.

**LifeWay Worship** has long been a provider of congregational music, but for decades in the form of hymnals, choral, and orchestral music. Launched at the same time as their most recent hymnal (2008), www.LifeWayWorship.com is an excellent online source for sheet music and recordings for thousands of songs. While some of their arrangements are original and geared for the "typical evangelical church," most are very accessible arrangements of popular worship song recordings. I'm especially fond of these songs from LifeWay Worship:

"I Need Thee Every Hour"

"Nothing But the Blood"

"Turn Your Eyes upon Jesus"

**Integrity/Hosanna** is the granddaddy source for modern worship music. If I gave you a representative list, it would include dozens, even hundreds, of songs. Instead, here are three you've possibly heard or sung:

"How He Loves"

"Hosanna" (Praise Is Rising)

"Great I Am"

Modern hymn writer **Keith Getty** launched his public songwriting in 2000 with one of the greatest hymns of the this century, "In Christ Alone." You may know a couple of others on this list as well:

"By Faith"

"The Power of the Cross"

"Speak O Lord"

Darlene Zschech was the face of **Hillsong Music** for its first couple of decades. The first Sunday I was in East Africa on my first overseas mission trip we heard "Shout to the Lord" coming out of a local worship gathering. This is global music.

"From the Inside Out"

"The Stand"

"Oceans"

**Vineyard** - launched in 1982 in Southern California with "Spirit Song" by pastor John Wimber, the song writing of this community exploded some time later with many familiar songs.

"Come, Now Is the Time to Worship"

"Breathe"

"One Thing Remains"

**Passion** - this movement focused on college students, raising up a generation that would change the world, was launched in 1997. Names associated include Louie Giglio, Chris Tomlin, Matt Redman, David Crowder, and many others.

"How Great Is Our God"

"Whom Shall I Fear"

"Even So, Come"


**Bethel Music** is an extension of Bethel Church and was just launched in 2009. Names you may recognize include Jeremy Riddle and Brian Johnson.

"This Is Amazing Grace"

"One Thing Remains"

"Forever" (We Sing Hallelujah)


**North Point** Church in Atlanta, GA has become the largest church in the US. Their worship ministry has been releasing strong songs for years by writers such as Steve Fee, Seth Condrey, and Todd Fields.

"No One Higher"

"Glory to God Forever"

"Death Was Arrested"


**Elevation Worship** is innovative and unique. Pastor Steven Furtick is often a part of writing songs that contribute to the worship series he preaches. If you've not yet become familiar, check out songs like the following:

"Unstoppable God"

"Only King Forever"

"Blessed Assurance"

**Vertical Church Band** is an expression of Harvest Bible Church in Chicago, IL. Names you may recognize include Meredith Andrews, Andi Rozier, and Mia Fieldes.

"Open Up the Heavens"

"Spirit of the Living God"

"Not for a Moment" (After All)

**Gateway Worship** features recording artists who worship leaders such as Kari Jobe and Thomas Miller.

"Revelation Song"

"Come Thou Fount, Come Thou King"

"Grace that Won't Let Go"

~

The next challenge is how to get those songs from those sources and into your church. Depending on the kind of musicians you have, there are two major streams of music: chord charts and written music. If you have both—like we do—it's just a bit more fun to work out.

If you use only chord charts, which means your folks learn by listening, you can get by with a single source for nearly all of your music: SongSelect by CCLI. Let's start with CCLI, or Christian Copyright Licensing Incorporated. If you print or project lyrics for any songs, a license is required to do so. CCLI was formed to make it possible for churches of all sizes to gain legal and ethical copyright permission to do this. If your church does not have a CCLI license, please take care of that before finishing this book. The fees are very reasonable and are scaled according to church size. You can find out more at www.ccli.com.

One of the helpful tools on the CCLI site is the "Top 100" songs, a list of the songs most churches sing most often. While I'm not advocating a consumeristic, pragmatic approach to song selection, I often find it helpful to look over the list and make sure I'm not missing a great song that "everybody else" is singing. Since my goal is to get as many people as possible engaged through the songs I choose, it only makes sense that the songs being sung the most all around the country can inform my song selection. (For international readers, CCLI tracks the song use by country, so this will hold in your part of the world as well.)

One branch of CCLI is called SongSelect, and for a very reasonable annual fee, you can download chord charts, lead sheets, vocal sheets (which look sort of like a hymnal), lyrics, and audio samples. This is a tremendous resource for churches who have people who learn to play and sing like rock musicians more than those traditionally trained.

Speaking of those traditionally trained, you may be in a more established church where you have musicians in need of written music, especially pianists and orchestral instrument players—flute, violin, cello, trumpet, etc. Even more than LifeWay Worship, PraiseCharts has become my go-to source for music like this. It is fairly costly until you look into memberships where you can buy and download a lot of songs (piano/vocal) or full orchestrations. Praise-Charts also offers chord charts, so if you have musicians who prefer that form, they can all play in the same sandbox. One benefit of PraiseCharts I've found is that they are essentially transcriptions of recordings. So, when you find a great version of a song, your team can use it as a reference point for the music from PraiseCharts. When they play/sing it, it will immediately sound similar to that recording.

~

Perhaps the most significant resource for church music since the hymnal, online worship planning has changed everything. There are a handful of such systems, including one at www.lifewayworship.com (LW). Many folks choose to use www.worshipplanning.com (WP). The most common tool in use these days is www.planningcenteronline.com (PCO). I encourage you to check them out. I'm most familiar with PCO, so let me share some of what it does for our worship ministry.

One of our servants gets an email from me via PCO. When they open it, responding is as simple as clicking the green "Accept" icon or the red "Decline" one. I schedule people as much as three weeks out.

If they are able to serve that weekend, and they click "Accept" on their phone, tablet, or computer, they are automatically connected to that order of service. Once there, they can view the service, see the print music/chord charts, hear a demo of each song, and use those tools to practice on their own before rehearsal.

For those who choose to download PCO's companion app, Music Stand, they can view the music for their part (chord sheet, lead sheet, piano part, flute part, etc.) in the service order on their iPad/tablet. The Music Stand app is even better for practice at home—they can play with a built-in metronome, the demo recording of the song, or on their own.

That's on their end. For the worship planner, it makes it easy to track song usage, how often people have been on the team, coordinate those who serve (we use vocals, band, tech, ushers, and other leaders), and I can even communicate specific notes about songs—who will lead out, who will accompany, changes to form, etc.

We use PCO to coordinate five services in two venues, involving more than 100 people. I can't imagine being able to do what we do without it. Online planning is a powerful tool for those who use it.

## ADVANCED RESOURCES

Multitracks - For you readers who are technology ori-
ented as keyboardists, drummers, or guitarists this may not
really be an advanced resource, but for many of us it is.
Nowadays when a worship song is recorded, the studio will
create stems or tracks for each instrument and vocal part.
There are companies who have made it possible for churches
to use these stems along with their live band. Here is a very
simple explanation: the drummer presses a button on a
computer (or a tablet or even a phone) and those in the band
who have in-ear monitors would hear a click track, including
a count in. The band plays with the click. Whatever tracks
from the recording that you don't have in your band—those
you really want to include for that song—playback along
with the click. While the click in only heard by the musicians, the rest of the sounds are heard by the congregation.
So you could have a Sunday where the bass player gets sick
and simply un-mute the bass channel on the stems. Voilá!
The congregation hears the original bass line. This can also
be great for things like drum loops, feature instrumental
lines (e.g., cello), and any "unusual" sound. However, because worship is primarily an incarnated event— led by
people for people—I'd counsel church leaders to use this
technology sparingly. (There is a free demo available at
www.multitrack.com.)

Ableton Live - If you'd like to control screens, lights, tempo of songs, use Multitracks (stems), and just about everything else, you might dive into Ableton Live. It is a phenomenal tool, and if you are on the tech-inclined side of worship ministry, I would highly suggest you check it out. (A free demo is available at www.ableton.com)

INDIVIDUAL CHALLENGE — Any of the above groups, songs, or resources with which you are completely unfamiliar, take a few minutes to explore. If you know them all, dive deep into the one that is least familiar.

GROUP CHALLENGE — Share your favorite resource with the group, especially if it isn't mentioned in this chapter. Talk about why you like that particular one.

GOING DEEPER — Explore these websites:

www.worshiptogther.com
www.leadworship.com
www.worshiphousemedia.com
www.allaboutworship.com

# 10 — EVALUATION AS A LEADER

We evaluate what we value. Even the words share a common root. This is true of our houses, our relationships, and our jobs. Since worship is at the core of the life of a church, it seems wise to evaluate it with great care. If it seems difficult to evaluate worship, that may be because we are evaluating people. That can be touchy, even risky. I would submit that it is worth the risk. God takes our worship of Him very seriously. And so, filled with grace and truth, let's consider some thoughts on how to evaluate worship.

At least three distinct segments should be evaluated:
1) Yourself
2) Your team
3) Your congregation

When someone comes to you and says, "Good job," or "Great worship," or "Excellent music" after you lead a song or a service, what do they mean? Is it possible to evaluate the effectiveness of your worship leadership? Of the worship experience?

In some basic ways, of course you can. Simple questions like these are a good place to start:

- Was I well prepared—spiritually, musically, relationally?
- Did I play the music accurately?
- Did I get the words right--singing and communicating them well?
- Did I engage my heart and my mind toward God rather than toward the music?
- Did I connect with the worshipers, seeking to help them connect with God?

Or, if you are a technician instead of a musician:
Did the microphones (and other audio cues, such as videos) work when they were supposed to?
Did the screens change ahead of the congregation at a good pace?

And, if you were the leader for the service:
Did I prepare the rest of the team well, both those on the platform and those in the tech booth—spiritually, musically, relationally?
Were there awkward moments of silence, or did things flow smoothly?

As a team, it would be helpful to gather after the service to ask some questions. You might do this between multiple services, very briefly after the service, or electronically within 24 hours of the service:

- Is there anything we should have done differently (song tempos, length, flow, transitions, etc.)?
- Is there anything we should do differently moving forward?

Now, how do we gather evaluative comments from the congregation? So much of what we hope happens in worship is not producible or predictable, let alone measurable. Can you gauge spirit and truth? Can you tell if people have connected their hearts and minds with the heart and mind of their Savior?

I believe you can. You simply have to ask.

You might begin doing this anecdotally. Start with those in the ministry but not on the team for the day. Ask your close friends and family some of these same questions. Don't be obnoxious about it by asking too much or too often, but seek feedback.

Once you think things are working reasonably well most of the time, you may develop a list of questions that resonate with the purpose, mission, and vision of your church—even more, with your worship ministry. See Appendix E for an example.

~

Let's return to the benefits of walking through this process. There is an overarching effect to evaluation, clarifying goals, and strengthening planning. Therefore, it will help greatly if you connect your evaluative questions to your goals.

For example, if a core goal of your worship ministry is to cultivate a sense of community, you might evaluate the language of your spoken and sung words: did you use both "I" and "we" language? Was the house lighting appropriate? Are you employing the stories of your people? If a goal is to consistently have prayer as part of your service, ask if the worshiper experienced it as a prayerful time.

Finally, if you value the concept of three audiences of worship—God, Church, and Unredeemed—go back and ask yourself (and your team) if all three were considered in planning and engaged in execution.

Evaluation isn't difficult or complicated, but it must be intentional. Develop a list of questions. Ask people from different demographics and preferences to answer those questions—perhaps for a month or for a series. Ask those who are supportive and those who are frustrated. These two groups can learn different things from the evaluative experience, both of which can serve your leadership long term.

INDIVIDUAL CHALLENGE — Identify five people to ask about the worship gathering in your church this Sunday. Think about different generations and different demographics. Come up with your own list of three to five questions. Then, ask. Don't "argue" with their feedback. Share any insights that seem significant to you with others on your team that will be encouraged and/or improved by the responses.

GROUP CHALLENGE — Use this as a team building exercise. Evaluate each other. Affirm three things each person in your group does well in their role as a worship leader/team member. Suggest one area for improvement. Do this with grace. Do everything with grace.

# APPENDIX A — USING THIS BOOK

We used this material on a series of Sunday evening meetings. Looking back, we agreed that the overall approach was great. We also agreed that some modifications would be very helpful. This is what our group ended up describing as ideal. So, we offer it to you as a plan you can implement, adapt, or use as a way to come up with your own approach.

Our church has a Sunday evening service (not the same as Sunday morning). We use that time as a chance to develop leaders. So our Worship Leader Academy (WLA) met at 5 pm to go over new material for that session, 5:30 pm to prepare two songs for the service, led the worship time at 6pm, then left the service to debrief how the music time went and to dig deeper into the material for the evening. Each chapter in this book represents two sessions of WLA. There were often times we wanted to be in the whole evening service, so we would meet an hour earlier to get more time in.

In general, 30 minutes of worship prep, 20 minutes of worship leading, and two hours of instruction and conversation. The outline we used is the following:

I. Leading Yourself
   A. Self Awareness
   B. Christ Awareness (Spiritual Disciplines; Soul Care)
   C. Relational Awareness (Pastoral Authority)
   D. Position Awareness (Strengths & Weaknesses)
   E. Fashion

II. Leading a Team
   A. Lovingly
   B. Spiritually
   C. Musically
   D. Relationally
   E. Clear Expectations

III. Leading with Vision
   A. Vision for PEOPLE not just SONGS/SERVICES
   B. Song (big, middle, little)
   C. Service (big, middle, little)
   D. Ministry (big, middle, little)

IV. Leading by Design
   A. Service Models
   B. Flow
   C. Transitions
   D. Song Choice - audiences of worship

V. Leading with Music
   A. Real World Music Theory
   B. Keys, Capos, and Context

VI . Leading with Technology
   A. Sound
   B. Video
   C. Lights
   D. Cameras

VII. Leading Great Rehearsals
   A. Have a plan - beginning, middle, ending
   B. Order of songs
   C. Be prepared
   D. Consider direction vs. collaboration

VIII. Leadership Resources (and Logistics)
   A. CCLI (copyright law and resources)
   B. PraiseCharts
   C. Online planning tools
   D. Multitracks
   E. Ableton Live

VIII. Evaluation
   A. How do you evaluate worship?
   B. How would you evaluate this Academy?

Before each session, the group had some homework to do. These students are busy people—full time students, employees, stay-at-home moms, and active at the church. For each session, there was less than an hour of homework assigned. The homework assignments came primarily from the sources listed at the end of each chapter under "Going Deeper." We also watched videos, shared a Facebook group for interaction, and communicated by email and text. This sense of community was fostered in the ways we prayed for one another and shared the journey by conversation in the classroom setting. Starting with self-leadership and the spiritual side of things really helped this dynamic. We enjoyed cheering each other on.

We suggest you take two road trips as a part of the WLA experience, one mid-year and one near the end. Attend a couple of worship gatherings at one or two churches each trip. Talk about the experience based on what you're learning. Meet with the worship pastor at one or both of those churches if possible, and ask them questions. If you're a drummer, talk with their drummer. If you run screens, check out how they do it. When possible, choose to attend a church that's just a step or two beyond your own, both in size and in worship style.

I can't overstate how valuable it is for those in your group (even if it is one on one) to lead worship and be given feedback on their leadership.

This "laboratory" element is where learning moves from intellectual to experiential. The students' questions get better, motivation gets stronger, and growth gets faster. If you have a full group, take turns as the point person. If you have a really large group, break into teams to each lead a song or a service.

If this approach serves you, please spread the word. Share with your friends. If everyone I know in ministry and everyone you know in ministry starts raising up worship leaders, we might catch up to the need. Lead and teach prayerfully. Our God will supply our need.

# APPENDIX B — CHAMPIONS ELITE ALL-STAR

**Teams Tryout Information**

Your child has shown interest in dancing for the Champions Elite All-Stars. The following is information on tryouts, practices, competitions, expenses, and the commitment it takes to dance for Champions. We do not want to discourage anyone from trying out; however, it is a very time consuming activity, and we expect full dedication from all who participate.

Tryouts
Your child must first tryout and be chosen to be on the team. The 2006-2007 All-Star teams will be as follows: Junior All-Stars grades 5-9 and Senior All-Stars grades 9-12. Every dancer must tryout.

| | | |
|---|---|---|
| Clinic (both Jr. & Sr.) | Sunday, April 23 | 5:00-7:00 |
| Clinic Review(optional) | Monday, April 24 | 7:00-8:00 |
| Tryout (both teams) | Thursday, April 27 | 6:30 |

There will be a mandatory parent meeting following the tryout. Time will be posted the day of, but probably about 7:30 when the names are posted. At this time you will be expected to fill out monthly withdrawal forms or pay in full for the year. All questions pertaining to the season will be addressed then.

If you cannot make the tryout date, you must make other arrangements with the coach and have a separate tryout. If you cannot attend a clinic your child must learn the material from another student on his or her own time.

I will be teaching a dance primarily consisting of pom and hip-hop. I am looking for dancers that pick up quickly and work hard. This routine should be clean, sharp, and fun to watch. I will also be looking at toe touches, splits, turns, and leap passes. If you have not previously learned these skills, it is nothing to worry about.

All details regarding tryout material/requirements will be explained/taught at clinics. Due to limited space, parents will not be permitted to attend clinics or tryouts. Results will be posted on the outside door of Champions approximately one hour after tryouts.

All students wishing to tryout will be required to fill out a tryout information agreement (enclosed) to be read and signed by the parents or legal guardians. THIS MUST BE COMPLETELY FILLED OUT AND SIGNED, OR YOUR CHILD CANNOT TRYOUT.

**Practices**
Squad members are expected to arrive 10 minutes early to practice. No parents, brothers, sisters, friends, or boyfriends will be allowed at practice. We will have open practice close to competition time for parents to come and watch. If you do

not like being asked to leave practice, please do not attempt to stay after practice has started.

There will be 1 or 2 practices a week beginning in May. During the summer I generally practice twice a week and during the school year once a week. Closer to competitions I do add extra practices as needed. Days and times have yet to be set. There may be times when additional individual practices are needed. Practices will be MANDATORY in August. If you must miss a practice during August, there is a possibility that you will not perform at the first competition.

Practices will be excused for the following reasons: illness, family vacations, and death in the family. School dance/cheer team practices, ball games, and competitions may be considered excused. However, this must be a revolving door. We will occasionally excuse team members for school cheer and dance functions as long as the school coach does the same for All-Star practices and competitions.

## Competitions

We plan on attending as many local competitions as possible this year. When we say local, we mean within 3-4 hour driving distance. Competitions attended may change. Please do not make airline reservations until a deposit on a Nationals trip has been made. We do not travel to competitions together. You will be responsible for your child and their transportation to competitions. Our competition season is September-March, and we try to do one competition a month. The following are a few competitions we have in mind:

Jamfest, Louisville Slugger Field
Hallojam, Evansville, IN
Cheersport Nationals, Atlanta
New York City Championships

ProCheer exhibitions
Local high school exhibitions

## Costs

Each dancer is required to pay monthly dues of $60. We require each dancer to pay for the 11 months of All-Stars at the start of the season ($660), OR to sign up to have $60 directly withdrawn from their parent's bank account on the first of each month. There are no other payment options. If you decide to pay by direct withdrawal, you will be asked to fill out paperwork and provide a voided check at the first parent meeting.

Each individual will be responsible for entry fees to competitions (most run about $15 to $75). Nationals will be considerably more. These fees will be due when requested. There will also be a $2-$5 fee attached to all entry fees collected for paperwork, postage, team mom, coaches expenses, etc. Uniform fees are approximate, and remember, you may fundraise to eliminate some of these costs.

Uniform  $200 (for both pom and hip hop, not each)
Shoes  $40
Practice clothes $50
Choreographer $150

I will be hiring a choreographer to come in for the hip-hop routines and possibly some locals to help with pom. It is becoming crucial to have great choreography in order to be competitive. Choreography fees will be due within the month of May. I will give exact amounts later.

Uniform fees are expected IN FULL when requested. These are typically spread throughout the summer months.

As you can see, the cost for your child to be a member of the Champions Dance team is a serious investment. You have monthly fees, entry fees, uniform costs, shoes, spirit packs, and travel/hotel expenses at some of the competitions we go to. Please take this into consideration before allowing your child to tryout.

Fundraising

Unlike school teams, fundraising is optional. Only those that work the fundraiser split the money. A "fundraising committee" may be started. I will not be on this committee. Parents will be in total control of fundraising; however, I must approve all ideas before they begin.

## Dismissal Policy

There will be no refund given to anyone who quits or who is dismissed from the team. Parents who complain constantly or cause general "uneasiness" on a team will only succeed in getting their child removed from the team. Champions reserves the right to cancel a student membership at any time.

Expectations

Squad members are expected to put their differences and individual concerns aside when they come to practice. We will not tolerate bickering between girls (or parents for that matter). Our decisions concerning placement of positions on the squad and in routines are final. We will do our best to use each girl to her full potential. Your skill performance at tryouts is expected the entire year and should only advance. Team members may be placed in alternate positions if they are not meeting routine expectations. Your concerns will be addressed, but again, our decisions will be final.

## Alternates

Alternates will be taken if needed. All fees and practices apply to alternates. Being an alternate simply means there are areas to work on. If I feel you are ready for a competition or performance, I will add you to that particular event. Alternates should not assume that because they are added to one performance that they will be added to future performances.

## Classes

Technique classes are offered throughout the year to work on technical skills such as leaps and turns. They meet once a week and are $7.50/group class (one hour) and $18.00/individual class (30 min.). Payment is expected the first class of every month and you pay for the month in full. If you miss a class you will be given an opportunity to make it up. Paying "by the class" is not accepted.

## Miscellaneous

Any questions not answered by the packet can be answered at the first parent meeting following tryouts. Please make sure that the last page of this packet is filled out properly before attending the tryout clinics.

If there are not enough kids to make a Junior team, those kids will be allowed to audition for the Senior team. Also, even if there are enough members to make a Junior team, I will probably be bringing someone in to help me coach that team this year.

## ALL STAR AGREEMENT

I have read and understand the rules and responsibilities that are expected of me should my child make the Champions All Star Dance Team. I understand that $660 is due for my child to dance for Champions. This amount will be paid up front or directly withdrawn from my account from May 2006 until March 2007. Should my child quit or be dismissed for any reason listed, I will not be given a refund and/or the monthly amount of $60 will continue to be withdrawn. I understand that should my child stop doing the required skills for the team, she/he will not be allowed to compete. "The Champions logo" and "Champions All Stars" apparel is property of Champions Elite Cheerleading and Dance. It is unlawful to have these reproduced.

Should my child need medical assistance and I cannot be reached, I give permission for the Champions staff to take my child to _____ hospital.

Parent Signature _____

Date _____

This form must be notarized.

Signature of Notary Public _____ Exp. Date _____

ALL STAR INFORMATION

Child's Name _____ Grade Entering ___

Parents' Names _____

Address _____ City _____ Zip _____

Phone Numbers (home and cell) _____

Email _____

Insurance Carrier _____

Policy Number _____

Emergency Contact/Phone _____

Are there any health conditions and/or medications that your child is taking that we should know about? Please list.


T-Shirt Size _____          Soffe Short Size _____

Sports Bra Size _____          Sweatshirt Size _____

# APPENDIX C — PLATFORM SERVANT GUIDELINES

Maintain the heart, mind, and attitude of a servant. If you ever need help with this, talk with a worship committee member or your worship pastor. Healthy people make healthy teams.

Respond to Planning Center Online (PCO) invitations within 48 hours. If it's not possible to make a decision that quickly, reply with an email (or other means) that you need more time. PCO invitations include rehearsal and service times. You are needed and expected at both. If you need more time to make a decision, put a reminder on your calendar to respond to PCO within the next 48 hours. If you have to decline an invitation, do so as soon as possible to give the worship leader time to find a replacement for that week.

Learn the songs. At a minimum, use PCO recordings to listen and/or sheet music to look at—whichever helps you learn better. Pay careful attention to the lyrics. Get a feel for the vibe of the song. Learn by listening. You can also watch videos, listen to other recordings of the songs to gain familiarity and give yourself ideas for creativity. That's not expected, but will help you grow as a worship leader.

Prepare to rehearse. The best worship gatherings, musically and technically, will not be as good as the best rehearsals. So, practice to the highest level possible. Strive to make practices flawless. When you come to worship rehearsal--we call it worship prep-- it is to put the pieces together, not to learn the music. We expect one another to learn the songs before we practice them together. (If you'd like help one-on-one before a rehearsal, ask the worship pastor.)

Bring your music to rehearsals and services. If you want/need music, either print your own copy or set up your iPad (or other tablet) to have the songs ready using the free Music Stand app available to use with PCO.

Be on time for rehearsal—this means ready to go-- tuned up, warmed up, hooked up, mic'd up, etc.--before the rehearsal begins. When you are missing or late, the rest of the team suffers. If you have to be late, alert the worship pastor or whoever is leading rehearsal that week.

Ask for help. If there is ANYTHING you need or want that will make it possible for you to do your job better, please ask. Your leaders are here to resource you, equip you, and encourage you. If we don't know what you need, we can't help.

If you have to step aside...If you cannot fulfill a service you've previously agreed to serve, let the worship pastor know immediately by text, email, or phone. Make sure you give ample time to whoever will fill in for you to be prepared.

Constantly improve. Do something every week to get better. Watch a video on YouTube or Ministry Grid. This can be a five-minute task or a full-blown classroom, workshop, or conference experience. Just keep improving. If you need suggestions, ask the worship pastor.

Aspire. Let's become the place where churches in our region send their teams to learn about how to make much of Jesus through worship leading.

## Instrumentalists

• As you're practicing on your own, pay close attention to the lyrics, and allow them to affect the way you play—section by section, phrase by phrase, and even at times, word by word.

• Play in worship prep the same way you'll play in worship. This is essential for the rest of the band but even more so for the sound technicians.

• Learn what you need to know about the way our sound system works, especially the ME-1 personal monitors.

• Know your music well enough to be able to get to Jesus through it.

**Vocalists**

• Learn the lyrics. You don't have to have them fully memorized, but you should look at the confidence monitor infrequently, not steadily.

• Sing in worship prep the same way you'll sing in worship. This helps the other singers and the band, but it is essential for the audio technicians.

• Sing with the microphone close to your mouth. You should be able to lick it, without actually doing so. This is important to enable our audio technicians to mix the vest best sound for the congregation. Remember, what you hear on stage isn't what they hear in the house.

• Learn what you need to know about the way our sound system works. For example, never point a microphone at the stage monitors.

• Be willing to speak up in worship prep and the run through so you can hear yourself and those around you.


**Common Expectations**

Here are the shared expectations across all groups in the worship ministry, including the choir. I hope these help us continually build one another up!

1) We will increasingly REFLECT* the image of Jesus;

2) We will have fun, and when we have fun, it will be because we're all having fun at the same time;

3) We will prepare well—in and out of rehearsals--so we can be free to worship;

4) We will start on time and end on time;

5) We will be here when we can, for rehearsals and for services. We will not feel condemned or guilty when we cannot be here. Those are lies from the pit of hell;

6) We will be *for* one another, encourage one another, and pray for one another;

7) We will delight in rehearsing, in praying, in learning, in community, and most importantly—in Jesus.

*REFLECT is WBC's discipleship strategy:

Relationship

Evangelism

Fruit of the Spirit

Listening

Edification

Christ-likeness

Transformation.

# APPENDIX D — COMMON MUSIC TERMS

*Ritard* or *Ritardando* - slow down

*Crescendo* - slowly get louder

*Decrescendo* - slowly get softer

*Diminuendo* - same as decrescendo

*Fermata* - hold the note 'til someone tells everyone else to stop

## Tempo

Beats per minute (BPM) - usually written at the beginning of a piece of music; this is how many beats of music—regardless of the time signature—happen in 60 seconds. You can download free metronome apps for your phone that will click the right number if you plug it in.

Time signatures - the top (or first) number is how many beats in a measure; the bottom number is what kind of note gets the beat.

2/4 = 2 quarter notes in a measure

3/4 = 3 quarter notes in a measure

4/4 = 4 quarter notes in a measure

6/8 = 6 eighth notes in a measure

Rhythm (when you add stuff to a note, it gets shorter)

Whole note - lasts the whole measure

Half note - 2 beats (half of a 4/4 measure, historically known as "common time")

Quarter note - 1 beat

Eighth note - 1/2 beat

Sixteenth note - 1/4 beat

Dynamics

*pp* - very soft (*pianissimo*)

*p* - soft (*piano*)

*mp* - medium soft (*mezzo-piano*)

*mf* - medium loud (*mezzo-forte*)

*f* - loud (*forte*)

*ff* - very loud (*fortissimo*)

*sfz* - suddenly loud (*sforzando*)

*accent* - emphasize the beginning of the note, making it a little louder

*tenuto* - stretch, or lean into a note

*staccato* - short, detached

"Road Map"

DC - the beginning (Da Capo literally means "the head")

DS - the sign (Del Signo)

Coda - tagged on to the end (literally means "tail")

Repeat - go back to the other repeat sign

Measure numbers - almost always found at the beginning of every line and often found at the bottom left corner of every measure.

# APPENDIX E — WORSHIP EVALUATION QUESTIONS

**Overarching Questions: Over the course of the month…**

1. …was opportunity provided to "worship in Spirit and Truth" (John 4) In other words, were both your heart and mind engaged? Share any memorable examples.

2. …was there a sense of both "I" and "we" (I meaning personal/individual and we meaning community/family)? Are there any examples that stand out?

3. …was there a clear attempt to build up Christ followers and connect those still far from God? Can you point to specifics?

4. …did prayer seem to be a significant part of both preparation and presentation of the services? Was there adequate time spent in prayer during the services? If not, do you have any suggestions?

**Series Questions: Over the course of the last month or so…**

1. …was the overall theme of the series evident in each gathering?

2. …how did we do at meeting the objective of this series?


**Service Questions: Over the course of the last month…**

1. …did the songs "work?" Were they effectively led? Do you remember any of them that should have been done differently? In a different place? Any specific suggestions?

2. …did the other worship elements (drama, video, prayer, reading, etc.) "work?" Should they have been placed differently? Written differently? Performed differently? Staged differently?

3. …was the general flow easy to go with, or were there bumpy moments? Any examples to offer?

4. …was each element of worship important to the overall experience, or did some seem extraneous (e.g. Drama, songs, videos, choral/solo piece, scripture reading)?

5. …was the music diverse, properly expressing the hearts of all generations? If so, how? If not, what was missing?

6. …how did the environmental elements (lighting, banners, decorations, stage props) contribute to the larger worship experience?

7. …were there any technical distractions? Anything we should have added?

**Lingering Questions? Over the course of the last month...**

1. ...was life change clearly offered? Do you remember how?

2. ...did life change occur?

(This question may not be able to be answered for a period of time.)

59918057R00086

Made in the USA
Middletown, DE
13 August 2019